Dear Colleague:

The extraordinary resource books in this series support our common goal as educators to apply best practices to everyday teaching. These books will encourage you to examine new resources and to discover and try out new and different teaching strategies. We hope you'll want to discuss and reflect on your strategies with other teachers and coaches in your support study group meetings (both face-to face and virtual) to make the most of the rich learning and teaching opportunities each discipline offers.

If we truly believe that all children can be successful in school, then we, must find ways to help all children develop to their full potential. This requires understanding of how children learn, thoughtful preparation of curriculum, reflection, adaptation of everyday practices, and ongoing professional support. To that end, the *Strategies for Teaching and Learning Professional Library* was developed. The series offers you countless opportunities for professional growth. Its rather like having your own workshops, coaching, and study groups between the covers of a book.

Each book in this series invites you to explore
- the theory regarding human learning and development—so you know why,
- the best instructional practices—so you know how, and
- continuous assessment of your students' learning as well as your own teaching and understanding—so you and your students know that you know.

The books offer *Dialogues* to reflect upon your practices, on your own and in study groups. The Dialogues invite responses to self-evaluative questions, experimentation with new instructional strategies in classrooms, and perhaps a rethinking of learning philosophy and classroom practices stimulated by new knowledge and understanding.

Shoptalks with short, lively reviews of the best latest professional literature as well as professional journals and associations.

Teacher-to-Teacher Field Notes full of tips and experiences from other practicing educators who offer different ways of thinking about teaching practices and a wide range of successful, practical classroom strategies and techniques to draw upon.

It's our hope that as you explore and reflect on your teaching practice, you'll continue to expand your teaching repertoire and share your success with your colleagues.

Sincerely,

Linda Adelman-Johannesen

Linda Adelman-Johannesen
President
The Galef Institute

The Strategies for Teaching and Learning Professional Library is part of the Galef Institute's school reform initiative *Different Ways of Knowing*.

Different Ways of Knowing is a philosophy of education based on research in child development, cognitive theory, and multiple intelligences. It offers teachers, administrators, artists and other specialists, and other school and district educators continuing professional growth opportunities integrated with teaching and learning materials. The materials are supportive of culturally and linguistically diverse school populations and help all teachers and children to be successful. Teaching strategies focus on interdisciplinary, thematic instruction integrating history and social studies with the performing and visual arts, literature, writing, math, and science. Developed with the leadership of Senior Author Linda Adelman-Johannesen, *Different Ways of Knowing* has been field tested in hundreds of classrooms across the country.

For more information, contact

The Galef Institute
11050 Santa Monica Boulevard, Third Floor, Los Angeles, California 90025
Tel 310.479.8883
Fax 310.473.9720
www.dwoknet.galef.org

Strategies for Teaching and Learning Professional Library

Contributors

President
Linda Adelman-Johannesen

Senior Vice President
Sue Beauregard

Editors
Resa Gabe Nikol
Susan Zinner

Editorial Consultant
Lois Bridges

Designer
Delfina Marquez-Noé

Photographers
Ted Beauregard
Dana Ross

The ideas and curricular frameworks in this book are the result of many conversations with other educators. My thanks go to Kaylene Yoder Ediger, Sandy Kaser, Leslie Kahn, Kathleen Crawford, Junardi Armstrong, and the teachers at Warren and Maldonado Elementary Schools. Jerry Harste, Carolyn Burke, and Kathryn Mitchell Pierce are long-distance collaborators who continuously challenge my thinking.

I owe my biggest thanks to Gloria Kauffman. Throughout the ten years we have been working together, Gloria has constantly pushed me to consider new perspectives and possibilities. Her willingness to think with me and to invite me into her classroom has allowed me to explore many of the ideas shared in this book. While books may be authored by one person, ideas are always co-authored. Gloria is a highly valued co-author. —KGS

Special thanks to Andrew G. Galef and Bronya Pereira Galef for their continuing commitment to our nation's children and educators.

Contents

Chapter 1

Bringing Literature into Your Classroom

Nine-year-old Darcy knows why reading and responding to "real books" make a difference in her learning and thinking. And it's the enthusiastic responses of children like Darcy that are encouraging teachers everywhere to bring literature into their classrooms. With their students, teachers are exploring literature as a way of knowing.

> This year, we read real books and we create our own learning through webbing, charting, and literature logs. I feel more comfy without workbooks. I am thinking more.

> This year we are all teachers and learners together, meaning that the teacher gives us ideas and we give the teacher ideas.

> We don't have levels of reading. We are all valued equally and our thinking is valued. Here everybody is equal. We can all read books and talk about them with each other in literature circles. Some people might take longer to read a book, but everybody does it and everybody has something to say.

Although we have always included children's literature in our classrooms, literature is now becoming an integral part of our curriculum. We are attending workshops, reading articles about literature-based curriculum, and bringing what we learn into the classroom.

SHOPTALK

Huck, Charlotte, Susan Hepler, Janet Hickman and Barbara Kiefer. *Children's Literature in the Elementary School*, 6th ed. Madison, Wisconsin: Brown and Benchmark, 1997.

This detailed reference book belongs on every teacher's desk. It examines the role of literature in children's lives, genres of children's books, and literature programs. Huck provides extensive bibliographies, genre and thematic groupings of books, and evaluation criteria for different kinds of books.

When thinking about the potentials of literature, a good start is to reflect on our personal histories as readers. Considering my childhood experiences helped me understand my attitudes toward reading as a teacher and how these attitudes related to those of my students. Books have always been an important part of my life. Growing up in a rural area with few neighbors, I made books my friends. They opened up many new ideas and worlds, transporting me beyond my family and community. Taking advantage of any available moment to read, I kept books with me all the time: My second-grade teacher tells the story of catching me sliding a library book out of my desk and sneaking a look between writing my spelling words on the weekly test!

My parents rarely read to me and couldn't afford to buy books, so I often went to the library. Most of the books I read, I found on my own, usually discovering a series—*Nancy Drew, the Bobbsey Twins,* or *Childhood Biography*—and reading down the whole shelf. When I was in sixth grade, I came upon several volumes of fairy tales at a neighbor's house and devoured them. I didn't know such stories existed and was enthralled with the fantasy worlds and the themes of good versus evil.

Still, I don't recall teachers reading to me or encouraging me to read until I was a senior in high school and took a course on "great" novels.

But by the time I was a college student, I had stopped reading for pleasure. I had so many textbooks to read that I associated reading with studying difficult, uninteresting books. It wasn't until I took a children's literature course as a preservice teacher that I rediscovered the joy of reading a good story simply because that story added something to my life.

As an adult, I always have a book with me in case I have to wait somewhere. Worrying that I might get caught on an airplane without anything to read, I carry twice as many books as I need. My home is filled with stacks of books waiting to be read—children's literature, professional books, mystery novels, and biographies.

DIALOGUE

What kinds of memories do I have about books and reading as a child, both at home and at school?

_____

_____

What kind of reader am I as an adult? How do I see my early experiences at home and at school influencing my reading attitudes and habits now?

_____

_____

How do my experiences as a child compare with those of my students?

_____

_____

Reasons To Read

As I reflect on my own story as a reader and listen to other teachers tell their stories, I realize that we read many different types of books and reading materials for a wide range of purposes. We read for amusement and for entertainment. We also read to obtain information, to learn, and to expand our learning lives. These reflections helped me explore ways students could experience these authentic purposes for reading.

S H O P T A L K

Short, Kathy, ed. *Research and Professional Resources in Children's Literature: Piecing a Patchwork Quilt.* Newark, Delaware: International Reading Association, 1995.

Classroom teachers, librarians, and university educators compiled this research on children's literature. The first section highlights the last ten years' trends and research, the second section lists professional journals, and the last section contains brief descriptions of professional books about children's literature. This valuable guide will help you locate research on a particular topic, strategies for using literature, and subject-specific children's books.

Reading should be life work, not just school work.

Stories Worth Reading

Reading is devalued if the books we read are not worth the effort of reading—when what we read adds nothing of significance or importance to our lives. Reading should be life work, not just school work. Students can discover the many pleasures of reading when they are treated to books with authentic, rich language, and convincing stories about life. Students connect with the themes of longing and belonging in *Sarah, Plain and Tall*, Patricia MacLachlan's story of a mail-order bride who longs for the sea, and of two children who long for a mother. The lyrical simplicity and rhythm of the language in this story draws readers into the powerful yearnings of the characters. Children can identify with Max when he is naughty and sent to his room in Maurice Sendak's *Where the Wild Things Are*. They fly with him on his journey of imagination and return home to forgiveness and a hot supper.

Field Notes: Teacher-To-Teacher

I read aloud to my students, introduced authors, and required outside reading. I also placed books around the room. But some of my methods did not support a love of reading. I demanded that book reports be written. I insisted that students read books I considered "good," but that seemed dated to them. I was not familiar with enough current children's literature to match books to my students' interests and reading ability. Week after week, we read short stories from the basal readers—contrived stories designed primarily to teach vocabulary. I knew my approach to books and the teaching of reading needed to change. I made the decision to use "real" books as the foundation for all areas of study in my classroom, and to search for ways to help my students respond and connect to these books.

Sandy Kaser
Robins Elementary School
Tucson, Arizona

Personal Connections to Life

Charlotte Huck (1990) helps us understand that literature is both a mirror and a window on life. As readers discover other experiences through literature, they find themselves reflected in books.

I learned the power of personal connections when I read aloud *The Pinballs* to a group of ten year olds in Indiana. This compelling novel by Betsy Byars is the story of three foster children who feel they have no control over their lives. Begging me to read more than just one chapter each day, children living in difficult family situations were immediately drawn to this book. Derrick and Kerry later read the book on their own—the first time either of them had ever *chosen* to read a book. And children who lived in strong, nuclear families gained new perspectives from this book about the experiences of some of their classmates.

Transforming Our Lives

Literature has the potential to transform children's lives. Charlotte Huck (1990) believes that literature connects the heart and mind. In schools, we often focus on knowledge and the mind, and fail to connect with the whole of our students' lives. Literature helps to reconnect feelings and thinking.

Gloria Kauffman read aloud Jane Yolen's *The Devil's Arithmetic* to her fifth graders at Maldonado Elementary School in Tucson, Arizona. Through this story of a modern child who goes back in time and finds herself taken away to a concentration camp, students learned about the Holocaust and lived within that time period, feeling the characters' struggles and triumphs. Knowing and feeling came together for the students.

The Great Kapok Tree captivated Junardi Armstrong's second graders at Cragin Elementary School in Tucson, Arizona. Written by Lynne Cherry, this provocative picture book tells a story of animals who depend on the rain forest for their existence. In a dream, they speak to the man who has come to cut down their trees. This book helped children go beyond facts about rain forests and get into the ethical and social issues involved in their destruction.

Illustration from *The Great Kapok Tree*, ©1990 by Lynne Cherry, reproduced with permission from Harcourt Brace and Company.

Field Notes: Teacher-To-Teacher

This summer we read a nonfiction book about butterflies that led five-year-old Jennifer into a butterfly research project. Later, we read a collection of stories written by children in a homeless shelter and, again, the book moved Jennifer into action. Through observing my child's and my own reading experiences, I realize what I had suspected for some time—we read in order to change ourselves and thereby to expand our potential to change the world.

Kathryn Mitchell Pierce
Glenridge Elementary School
Clayton, Missouri

Quality informational books are written from the perspective of one enthusiast sharing with another. Unlike textbooks, these informational books connect the heart and mind—and "light fires" in our minds.

Literature expands our life spaces. Taking us outside the boundaries of our life experiences to other places, time periods, and ways of living, literature helps us see that there are other ways to live our lives. Through reading, children discover peer groups that extend beyond the ones in their neighborhoods. They come to know literary children in books such as Michele Surat's *Angel Child, Dragon Child*, a picture book about a Vietnamese girl who is teased by her classmates, and Katherine Paterson's *Bridge to Terabithia*, a novel in which imaginary play develops into a friendship between two misfit, lonely children. Reading these books, children realize that there are a variety of ways that people can live together in harmony. They learn that different cultures have different ways of thinking about and living in the world.

Literature also stretches our imagination and encourages us to go beyond "what is" to "what might be." Living in a world with so many problems, we may tend to give up hope and overlook possibility for change. Literature invites us to consider "what if." For generations, hope and imagination have made it possible for children to be resilient and rise above their circumstances. Literature, like *The Giver* by Lois Lowry, *Grab Hands and Run* by Frances Temple, and *The Story of Jumping Mouse* by John Steptoe, encourages our children to hope and strive for other possibilities in their lives. *The Giver* uses the futuristic setting of a supposedly utopian community where all conflict has been eliminated. *Grab Hands and Run* is set in today's world and follows a family who tries to leave El Salvador after the father disappears.

The Story of Jumping Mouse is a Great Plains Indian narrative about a mouse who jeopardizes his own dream to help others in need. In each of these stories, the characters face desperate situations without giving up hope.

Above all, literature has the power to transform. As we read, we experience the lives of others in different times and places, and we carry these experiences back into our own worlds and view our lives differently. As Gloria Kauffman's student Mardell puts it, "I think about the problems that our world faces and I notice how authors solve the problems in their storybook worlds. I am a serious reader struggling for answers to solve my personal problem—my sister."

What Shall I Read?

As we read, we experience the lives of others in different times and places, and we carry these experiences back into our own worlds and view our lives differently.

Choice is essential to learning. Through choice, learners are able to make connections to interests and experiences that are significant to them. They take ownership of their learning. When students can choose what they read and how they will respond to it, reading becomes a meaningful experience in their lives. In every classroom, we find students with a wide range of interests, needs, and experiences. If all our students are going to find themselves in books and view the world from new perspectives, they need access to a wide variety of literature. Of course, no literature anthology or book list, no matter how carefully put together, can meet all the needs of a specific group of children. While historically, the availability of reading materials was a problem, today, the accessibility of excellent children's books is overwhelming.

S H O P T A L K

Goodman, Kenneth S., Patrick Shannon, Yvonne B. Freeman and Sharon Murphy. *Report Card on Basal Readers*. Katonah, New York: Richard Owen, 1988.

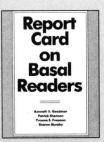

Shannon, Patrick and Kenneth Goodman. *Basal Readers: A Second Look*. Katonah, New York: Richard Owen, 1994.

In these two volumes, university and teacher researchers report on their work examining basal readers. Their research indicates that the language of these stories has often been simplified, illustrations frequently changed or omitted, and chapters taken out as excerpts from longer books. The researchers also analyze teachers' manuals, testing, and multicultural literature.

Many of my colleagues have discovered that the wider the variety of literature they introduce into their classrooms, the greater the range of books their students will pick up and read. These teachers have also learned that an imagined "instructional reading level" has little meaning when students can choose from all sorts of books. As adults, we don't limit ourselves to reading books from a specific instructional reading level. We read books that range from easy to difficult. The difficulty has as much to do with the match between the content of the book and our own experiences as it does with the linguistic difficulty of the book.

Without question, all readers need strategies for reading many kinds of books. Instead of "protecting" children—forcing them to read at a specific level—we need to give them the opportunity to read easy books to develop fluency, as well as difficult books where they must work to construct understandings. Learning to handle a range of difficulty enables readers to develop strategies for reading all kinds of books. We handicap children and prevent them from developing the strategies they need when we insist that they read only at their "instructional" level. Truly, there is no such thing as a "level" for reading. In the *Phi Delta Kappan* article "Reading Level: A Metaphor That Shapes Practice," Kenneth Cadenhead argues that instructional reading level is a misguided, artificial concept created by educators who didn't understand the reading process or how children learn to read.

SHOPTALK

Smith, Frank. *Reading Without Nonsense*, 3rd ed. New York: Teacher College Press, 1997.

In *Reading Without Nonsense*, Frank Smith examines the process of reading, the perceptual and language skills involved, and how nonreaders perceive the task of learning to read. He argues a simple truth—only through reading do children learn to read. For him, reading is not a visual, mechanical process composed of isolated skills that need to be pulled out and taught to children, but a process of constructing meaning, using a variety of cueing systems. Children don't learn to read and then read to learn. Even as new, developing readers, their focus should be on reading to learn.

While issues of illiteracy pervade the national press, I believe that *aliteracy*—when literate people *choose* not to read—is a more significant problem. American Book Industry statistics (Cramer and Castle 1994) tell us the extent of the problem. The statistics show that eighty percent of the books are read by only ten percent of the American population. In a survey of adult readers, forty-five percent of American adults said they had not read an entire book since finishing school. These adults learned to read in school, but they never came to appreciate reading as a way of knowing. Now, they read when necessary for their work or to get information, but they lack the desire to read. Because they don't value reading, their own children, in turn, will not be read to at home and the cycle of aliteracy may continue.

Literacy for the Future

Recently, the International Reading Association and the National Council of Teachers of English released a set of standards for the English Language Arts (1996). They set forth a vision of excellence while inviting further discussion about the fundamental goals of schooling and literacy.

These standards are based on three core beliefs:

- The ways that we use language to communicate and think are changing with new demands from technology and society. Our definition of "basic" must be expanded to prepare students for the literacy requirements of the future, as well as the present.

- We need a shared vision of this new, more rigorous literacy, as well as the support of parents and communities to help students realize this vision.
- To prepare all students to become literate citizens, we must hold high expectations for every student and every school.

The standards are learner-centered, and focus on the ways students actively participate in their learning and acquire knowledge through literacy and language. The interrelationships of what, why, and how students use reading, writing, listening, and speaking are considered the core of language arts programs in schools.

Several of the twelve standards in the document stress the importance of students reading a wide range of literature for different purposes. Students read to acquire new information, respond to the needs of society, build an understanding of human experience, and fulfill personal needs. According to the standards, a literate person must have a wide repertoire of strategies to comprehend, interpret, evaluate, and appreciate texts. Proficiency in these strategies, however, is not enough. A literate person must also participate as a knowledgeable, reflective, creative, and critical reader within literacy communities.

To reach these high standards, students need to use books and other reading materials for meaningful purposes, instead of filling in worksheets, copying words from the board, and answering questions from textbooks. The standards envision classrooms where students use literacy to solve real problems and to communicate with real audiences.

S H O P T A L K

International Reading Association and National Council of Teachers of English. *Standards for the English Language Arts.* Newark, Delaware: International Reading Association and Urbana, Illinois: National Council of Teachers of English, 1996.

This document includes an involved discussion of the twelve standards and the learning theories supporting them. Both the NCTE and the IRA are publishing additional books to support classroom teachers in realizing these standards. NCTE has an excellent *Standards in Practice* series that offers practical resources for classroom teachers in grades K-12.

Whether our students feel the powerful potentials of literature depends on how we use literature in our classrooms. When our students read real books, they discover stories that sustain and excite their minds. Literature is not a reward for finishing other class assignments, it is the content of reading. If students are able to read and respond to literature within a curriculum that is constructed around themes and student inquiry, books take on new life. Through literature, students can make the connections that lead to powerful learning and meaning-making. In the next four chapters, we will explore how to create a curriculum that supports literature as a way of knowing.

Literature is not a reward for finishing other class assignments, it is the content of reading.

S H O P T A L K

Sorensen, Marilou and Barbara Lehman, eds. *Teaching with Children's Books: Paths to Literature-Based Instruction.* Urbana, Illinois: National Council of Teachers of English, 1995.

Written by teachers, administrators, and teacher educators, this book focuses on the authors' practical experiences in moving from basal readers toward teaching and learning through children's literature. The chapters are organized around eight steps on the pathway to using literature in the classroom—understanding, considering, preparing, modeling, teaching, collaborating, assuming, and supporting.

Chapter 2

The Roles Literature Plays

In this chapter, we will think about our lives as teachers and how literature can become a way of knowing. This focus on literature and curriculum assumes that we share John Dewey's belief that teachers are decision-makers who construct curriculum with their students. We use the work of outside experts and the content of district and state curriculum to inform, not to determine our decisions.

When I first introduced literature into my classroom, I viewed it as a better way to teach students to read and write. While literature certainly fulfills this role, it has many more possibilities within the classroom. As I worked with students, I identified four roles for literature in the classroom. Literature is a way to

1. learn language
2. explore content area
3. know the world
4. critique the world.

Reading as a process of inquiry connects all of these roles. Although we read for enjoyment, we also read because it helps us find answers to the questions that matter to us in our lives, both in and out of school.

Literature as a Way To Learn Language

Many of us are exploring ways for our students to use literature as a way to learn language. As students read, they naturally learn about written language—how it's put together, how it works to convey meaning, and how specific, meaning-making strategies help them as readers and writers.

We can put literature to work in our writing workshops. As we invite our students to read and enjoy a range of children's authors, they naturally discover different writing styles and begin to develop their own writing strategies. As Frank Smith (1988) reminds us, every time we open the pages of a book, we receive lessons on how to write. Published authors show our students how to find a topic, start a story, use dialogue, and revise for an audience. And as our students participate in genre studies, discovering the unique complexities of historical fiction, mystery thrillers, or poetry, they begin to understand how language itself works.

S H O P T A L K

Harwayne, Shelley. *Lasting Impressions: Weaving Literature into the Writing Workshop.* Portsmouth, New Hampshire: Heinemann, 1992.

Packed with teaching ideas on how literature can support children in writing workshops, this book is a "must" for elementary school teachers. With a personal perspective, Harwayne follows one class over the course of a school year and includes many examples of children's work. Topics covered include ways to use literature to build classroom community, keep a writer's notebook, find writing topics, encourage careful listening, and inspire lifelong investigations into writing.

Leslie Kahn grew weary of the endless "shopping mall" and "gang" stories that her sixth-grade students at Warren Elementary School in Tucson, Arizona, wrote. Aiming to stir their creative juices, she introduced them to authors of informational books, such as David Macaulay, Aliki, and Mitsumasa Anno. These authors write on a wide range of topics in styles that engage readers with the use of direct and vivid language. They also combine text with different illustration techniques and creative book formats that add to both the readers' interest and the information in the text.

After their introduction to informational books, students formed literature circles—small discussion groups of usually less than five students. They talked about their personal connections to and interpretations of the books, and they also discussed the variety of topics, formats, and styles, and how they

might use these ideas in their own writing. Then the students moved to a genre study of poetry, discussing both the meaning of what they were reading and the writing strategies they too could use. After the genre studies, students enthusiastically tried other styles in their writing.

As students read, it is natural that at times they focus on their reading and writing strategies.

Literature can also help students reflect on and revise their reading strategies. Roxanne Lung and Clay Connor questioned whether their fifth-grade students at Maldonado Elementary School in Tucson, Arizona, were developing effective reading strategies for informational books. After talking with their students, they realized that many had only read narrative stories and weren't sure how to approach an expository text. So, to help their students learn how to read informational books, they held brief strategy discussions. As the students read historical informational books and biographies related to their inquiries on the Civil War, the teachers invited them to talk about the strategies they were using to understand these books. Students discussed how to make predictions, ask questions, and connect to their own ideas and experiences as they read. They also analyzed the organization and structure of these books.

As students read, it is natural that at times they focus on their reading and writing strategies. In addition, students may notice that the illustrations help create meaning, especially when they are reading picture books. Since art and written language are essential to the telling of the story in picture books, readers must successfully read both art and print to construct meaning from these books.

As her class was studying the environment, Gloria Kauffman and her third graders at Maldonado Elementary School in Tucson became intrigued with the work of a number of picture book illustrators—Peter Parnell, Lynne Cherry, and Jeannie Baker, to name a few. With different artistic styles and media, these illustrators all create fiction and nonfiction picture books that highlight nature. Using book sets they had put together, the students closely examined the works of these illustrators. Kauffman developed a studio time where students could do their own explorations of watercolor, pen and ink, and collage. Through these studio experiences and the illustrator text sets, children learned how to talk about art elements (color, line, light and dark, space, and shape) and art techniques (watercolor, collage, and pen and ink) that communicate particular meanings.

Discussions about language and art have a place in a literature-based classroom, particularly when students are experiencing difficulty as readers or when they need specific writing or illustrating strategies for their own work. The dominant focus, however, is not on strategies but on meaning itself—what students are learning about their lives and the world through books. Learning about reading and writing helps students learn about the world through language. Reading strategies are not of value in isolation from meaning-making.

Literature as a Way To Explore Content

We can help our students explore content area topics when we organize literature experiences around themes and topics in our studies of science, social studies, mathematics, and the arts.

We can help our students explore content area topics when we organize literature experiences around themes and topics in our studies of science, social studies, mathematics, and the arts. Students can discuss literature in relation to these topics, noting how it compares to their learning from other sources.

SHOPTALK

Whitin, David and Sandra Wilde. *Read Any Good Math Lately?: Children's Books for Mathematical Thinking, K-6.* Portsmouth, New Hampshire: Heinemann, 1992. Also *It's the Story That Counts: More Children's Books for Mathematical Learning, K-6.* Portsmouth, New Hampshire: Heinemann, 1995.

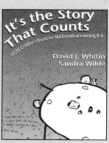

These two books provide many practical examples of how books portray mathematics as a tool for making sense of our world. Drawing upon a wealth of books and using samples of children's work, the authors explain the use of books to explore mathematical concepts, the importance of children's spontaneous reactions, and the role of mathematical conversation. The chapters are organized around common mathematical concepts with useful, annotated lists of children's books and mathematical explorations.

Gloria Kauffman and her fourth graders used literature as part of a nature unit that included a field trip to a local environmental center (Kauffman and Short 1990). Beginning the unit, she read aloud survival novels such as Gary Paulsen's *Hatchet*, a contemporary story of a boy's survival after a plane crash in the Canadian wilderness, and Scott O'Dell's *Island of the Blue Dolphins*, the historical story of an Indian girl who lived alone on a California island for eighteen years. As students listened to these books, they talked about how the characters found ways to survive by living with nature. They also met in small groups to discuss other survival novels—Paula Fox's *Monkey Island*, set among the homeless in New York City, Jean Craighead George's *My Side of the Mountain*, in the wilderness of the Catskills, and *Julie of the Wolves*, in the Alaska tundra.

S H O P T A L K

Saul, Wendy and Sybille Jagusch, eds. *Vital Connections: Children, Science, and Books.* Portsmouth, New Hampshire: Heinemann, 1991.

In *Vital Connections*, chapters by well-known science authors and educators offer methods for evaluating science books and using these books more effectively in libraries and classrooms. This book also describes how science books invite children into their pages through personal connections, creating a special relationship between the children and the books.

After finishing their discussions of these novels, students met in small groups to explore text sets on environmental issues. The sets included five to ten different picture books of fiction, nonfiction, and poetry related to a specific topic—erosion, plants, rocks, or glaciers. As the students met in their groups, they first read and discussed the various books in their sets. Kauffman then introduced the concept of student-inquiries, inviting her students to design their own experiments for investigating the ideas and information related to their focus. Later, each group set up a learning center so other class members could learn about their topic before visiting the environmental center.

Sandy Kaser (1994) invited her fifth-grade students to explore family histories through literature engagements and interviews with family and community members. They began by reading text sets of family stories focusing on fathers, mothers, brothers, sisters, and grandparents. During their discussions of these sets, students shared their personal family stories. Their interest in these stories led them to interview their own families and publish "remember when" stories in a classroom collection. Because many of the students shared stories about their younger days, they also chose to create time lines of their lives.

The students' interest in their own histories progressed to a class focus on biography and the lives of famous people. After creating a class timeline from these biographies, students decided to research the last one hundred years of their families. Many of the family stories they collected for this timeline connected to important events in American and Mexican history. Because these stories often involved wars, groups of students studied different wars through the use of informational books, as well as family and community interviews.

S H O P T A L K

Tunnell, Michael and Richard Ammon, eds. *The Story of Ourselves: Teaching History Through Children's Literature*. Portsmouth, New Hampshire: Heinemann, 1993.

Authors of children's historical books and public school and university educators wrote this informative book to offer support for teachers who want to use literature to create a history/social studies curriculum. Of special interest is a section called "Practical Applications" with in-depth classroom examples and an extensive bibliography of children's books.

Since her students were so interested in time lines, Kaser read aloud *My Place* by Nadia Wheatley and Donna Rawlins, a book that follows the changes over time in one place in Australia. The story inspired students to do further research about changes in their families and communities. They later met in literature circles to discuss novels about families from diverse cultures. Students read Paul Pitts's *Racing the Sun*, about a Navajo family's tensions over life on the reservation and in the city, Jerry Spinelli's *Maniac Magee*, about homelessness and racial prejudice in the city, and Yoshika Uchida's *A Jar of Dreams*, about the burden of the Depression and the prejudice toward Japanese Americans. Through their research and reading, they explored issues related to family, culture, and world conflict.

Literature as a Way To Know the World

Literature is itself a content area and a way to know the world. It differs from other ways of knowing such as science or history. Ralph Peterson and Mary Ann Eeds (1990) and Karen Smith (1990) have been instrumental in helping us understand this perspective. They argue that we've been so busy using literature for other purposes that we lost sight of literature having value in and of itself. In *The Reader, the Text, and the Poem*, Louise Rosenblatt asserts that through literature, readers are able to experience life in different ways. Literature enables them to live inside the world of the story in ways that transform their thinking about their lives and world.

Literature is itself a content area and a way to know the world.

If we need justification to simply read and enjoy literature, Rosenblatt provides it. She helps us understand that our students shouldn't always have to respond to literature through discussions, writing, or theme unit integrations. Students need time to read for the pure joy of it, during independent read-

ing when they have a wide choice of books. Instead of participating in a structured learning event, students may share their excitement about these books during informal class meetings.

Students can experience literature as a way of knowing when they talk about their "lived-through" experiences and personal connections in literature circles. Because everyone in a literature circle reads the same book, they can focus on their different interpretations and responses to the story, and look closely at literary elements such as character and theme. In a literature circle on Jean Craighead George's *Julie of the Wolves*, sixth graders in Kaylene Yoder Ediger's classroom in Millersburg Elementary School in Goshen, Indiana, explored themes of survival, death, communication, and culture. In addition, they discussed information about Alaska, wolves, and Eskimo cultures. They also debated their differing interpretations of the book's ending (Kauffman and Yoder 1990).

Tucson teacher Pamella Sherman invited her first graders at Warren Elementary School to study Tomie de Paola as an author/illustrator. The children discussed their personal connections to de Paola's stories and compared his stories across different themes, topics, and characters. They also conducted an analysis of his illustration style as they attempted to understand how it conveys meaning.

In both classrooms, these books were read and discussed, not because they were part of a particular theme unit, but because they related to children's personal inquiries of literature as a way of knowing about the world. The children were swept up in understanding how these books related to their lives.

S H O P T A L K

Peterson, Ralph and Maryann Eeds. *Grand Conversations: Literature Groups in Action.* New York: Scholastic, 1990.

This small book celebrates dialogue as a tool for responding to literature. Peterson and Eeds outline a literature program that has four basic components—story in the home (the beginning of the study of story), read-aloud, extensive reading, and intensive reading. In addition, the authors show us how to respond by considering a story's literary elements, such as plot, character, place, mood, and symbol. They also explain how to use a variety of assessment strategies to determine our students' comprehension of and involvement with literature.

Literature as a Way To Critique the World

Literature can also be used as a way to critique the world, particularly in relation to social, political, and cultural issues. Critical theorists urge us to consciously examine how our thinking is influenced by the community and world in which we live. They encourage us to examine issues such as homelessness, prejudice, cultural diversity, and living peacefully with others. By doing so, we may come to understand the problems of the world around us in new ways, to examine our histories in order to find our own voices, and to take action in changing our society. Literature helps us reflectively and critically think about the world in other ways, and look at our histories in relation to global complexities. Paulo Freire (1987) says that this critical consciousness is a way to reclaim one's voice, history, and future.

Field Notes: Teacher-To-Teacher

I am convinced that no newspaper or magazine article, no discussions of current events or TV news program could have had the impact that literature had on my students. At a young age, they experienced the lessons that history teaches at a level that had personal significance for them. They were able to bring these lessons into the present to support their changing understanding of society's frequently precarious future. David said to me one day, "Didn't they say that if you don't—something about Hitler. If you don't remember history and stuff about it that something will happen to you?" I asked him whether he meant that if you don't remember history that you are condemned to repeat it. "Yeah, that's it. I think that's true," he concluded.

Caryl Crowell
Borton Primary Magnet School
Tucson, Arizona

Literature helps us reflectively and critically think about the world in other ways, and look at our histories in relation to global complexities.

Caryl Crowell (1993) teaches a third-grade bilingual class at Borton Primary Magnet School in Tucson, Arizona. During the Gulf War, a small group of her students became concerned about war. To help them work through their fears and concerns, she put together a text set of picture books on war. Students read and discussed the books, most of which dealt with World War II. Through their discussions, they made many connections to the Gulf War and looked more critically at what was happening. Newspaper accounts had acquainted them with the technical aspects of war, but literature allowed them to consider human suffering and the psychological and social aspects of war as well.

Tucson, Arizona, teacher Kathleen Crawford works with a culturally diverse group of fourth graders at Warren Elementary School. As her students discussed Mildred Taylor's *Roll of Thunder, Hear My Cry* in a literature circle, they focused on the prejudice experienced by the Logans, an African American family living in Mississippi during the Depression. Students also explored how they faced prejudice in their school and community and were often silenced like the Logan family. They talked about problems with the water quality and the lack of bike paths in their part of the city as compared to wealthier sections of Tucson. They discussed the names they had been called by others in the school and in the community. Through these talks, their relationships with each other changed in positive ways. Teasing and name calling in the classroom and on the playground decreased. During class discussions, they listened thoughtfully to each other's opinions.

DIALOGUE

What are the ways I currently use literature in my classroom?

_____

_____

Which of the four roles of literature are highlighted in my curriculum: literature as a way to learn language, literature as a way to explore content area topics, literature as a way to know the world, or literature as a way to critique the world?

_____

_____

Which roles are missing?

_____

_____

The children in these two classrooms used literature as a way to consider their own perspectives as well as the ideas of those around them. They discussed critical issues facing society and considered new beliefs and actions in their own lives.

Highlighting a Range of Roles

Obviously the four roles of literature are not mutually exclusive. More than one is present during any literature experience in a classroom. But at any given point in time, one of these roles may take center stage and revise the readers' understandings. The students who engaged in an author study of Mitsumasa Anno, for example, learned and thought differently than the students who discussed the text set on war. We decide which role to highlight

Field Notes: Teacher-To-Teacher

For a few years, I worked hard preparing appropriate guide sheets on characters, plots, and themes for my students to use as they labored through a text. These sheets let me know if the students read the text and gave me a grade for my grade book. Unfortunately, these sheets did nothing to help students understand the potential of a literary experience or help enrich their experience with the text.

As I moved away from "basalizing" the text, I swung to the other extreme. The students read voraciously, and whatever response they made was accepted and encouraged. If they read William Steig's *Sylvester and the Magic Pebble* and responded by making a rock collage, that was acceptable. It took me several years of experience, reading, studying, sharing, and reflecting to come to an understanding about how and why I wanted to use literature in my classroom.

Karen Smith
Phoenix, Arizona

depending on the goals of our curriculum and the needs of our students. When I first began to integrate literature into my classroom, I found it helpful to choose one of these roles—literature as a way to explore a content area—as a starting point. First I replaced the history textbook with historical fiction, biographies, and informational books. I later replaced the basal reader with high quality literature. Gradually, I found ways to incorporate the four roles of literature into my classroom.

The issue is not which role is *the* right role. All of them have a place within our classrooms. They offer different potentials for influencing children's lives and for encouraging children to make connections as they read. Over the course of the school year, you'll want to focus on all four roles. The next chapter describes curricular engagements that will help you explore these roles in your curriculum.

DIALOGUE

How can I integrate literature into my current curriculum?

_____

_____

Where can I begin exploring literature?

_____

_____

Which role would make a good starting point for me?

_____

_____

Chapter 3

Learning Language and Learning about Language

Literature comes to life when it's part of a broader thematic focus or tied to children's personal inquiries. And as we've discussed, children use literature for many purposes.

Linguist Michael Halliday conducted research that frames my understandings of the ways we can use literature to explore curriculum. Halliday studied the language development of his son Nigel from the moment he was born. In *Learning How To Mean* (1975), Halliday argues that children focus on the meaning of what they are trying to say, not on grammatical conventions. Eventually, children do learn the conventions, but only because those conventions help them communicate their meanings more effectively to others.

Halliday (1984) found that in any meaningful language event, children have the opportunity to learn language, learn about language, and learn through language. They learn language through the "doing" of language—talking, listening, reading, and writing. They learn about language as they explore how language functions and the conventions that support communication. They also learn through language as they focus on what it is they are learning. In this case, language just happens to be the tool they are using to learn about topics and questions that are important to them.

Halliday's research provided a framework that helped me rethink the need for particular types of learning experiences with literature. As teachers, our goal is to make sure that students are involved in learning events that center

around each of these three opportunities. We want to give them the opportunity to learn by reading extensively from many different books and materials. We also want to provide them with strategy lessons, student-teacher
conferences, and shared reading experiences where they can examine their
reading strategies and the nature and function of written language. Finally, we
know they need to use literature to explore content and questions that are
significant to them in theme units, inquiry groups, and literature circles.

The following figure reflects the framework I use to think about the types of
learning events that might be part of the curriculum. You will have others
to add to these circles—there is no one right set of engagements. What mat-
ters is that students experience all three aspects of language learning.

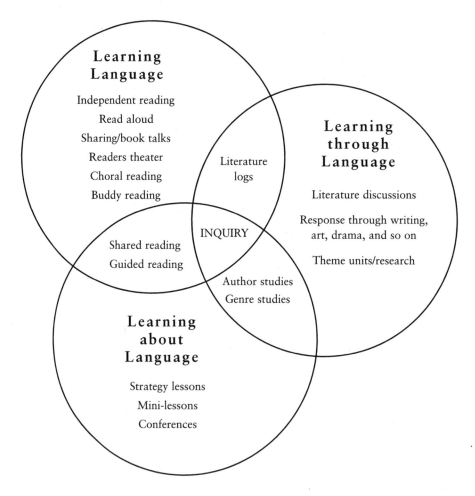

When I first brought literature into the curriculum, my goal was for children
to learn to love reading. I read aloud to them, set aside time for them to
choose and read books on their own, and planned fun projects with books.
Not surprisingly, my students came to enjoy books and became proficient
readers. But I also observed that while my students loved books, they did
not necessarily think deeply or critically about what they read. I had em-
phasized only one circle in the framework.

We progressed into learning through language when I introduced my students to theme units and literature circles. In literature circles, small groups of students read the same book and then met to discuss their understandings with each other.

Although students were involved in intensive literature discussions, I realized that they seldom had a chance to just read and enjoy a book without talking about it. I thought about myself as an adult reader—I discuss with others only a small portion of what I read. Reflecting on my teaching practices and reading habits helped me search for a better balance of intensive and extensive experiences so my students could learn language *and* learn through language.

I also realized that in moving away from the basal reader and skills worksheets, I had not found another way to help my students learn about language. My students needed support in developing strategies as readers and in thinking about how language functions. Before, I had overemphasized isolated skills, but completely eliminating learning about language was not the solution either. Based on my students' needs, I began teaching reading strategies—in short, focused lessons and student conferences.

All three aspects of learning language are essential in classrooms, but the balance among them varies according to student needs. In primary classrooms, for example, students must be given more time to read widely—choosing their own reading materials for enjoyment without structured learning events—and examine their reading strategies. However, while young children need predictable books and shared reading experiences to gain fluency, these books do not support an intensive consideration of meaning. We should, then, read aloud quality picture books that students can discuss in literature circles. This way, they'll discover that reading involves critique and inquiry.

In contrast, upper grade students spend most of their time learning content through reading, and rarely have time to simply enjoy a good book. They need to read widely and continue developing fluency and flexibility as readers. They also need to build on their reading strategies, especially for reading informational texts.

Many school districts and states are experiencing major pendulum shifts from one approach to another—from "book floods" to isolated skills approaches. Instead of arguing which one of these is "right," we need to create curriculum around what we know about language. Engagements that highlight learning language, learning about language, and learning through language all play essential roles in children's development as fluent and thoughtful readers.

In the remainder of this chapter, we will look at ways of using literature that help children learn language and learn about language. We'll see how children can learn through language in Chapter 4.

Engagements for Learning Language

Reading is a process. It is a process that offers readers the opportunity to learn more than just the story or information in front of them. Indeed, in reading many different kinds of materials and books, readers learn language and build a background of literature from which to make connections as they read other books. When students are able to read fluently from materials with highly predictable language, they begin to integrate reading strategies. Similarly, when they progress to more challenging reading, they develop strategies for dealing independently with "hard" books.

Read-aloud time, wide reading, partner reading, book talks and sharing, readers theater, and choral reading all encourage students to read. These engagements focus on the extensive reading and enjoyment of many books.

Reading Aloud to Students

Reading aloud and providing time for independent, self-selected reading are research and classroom-proven to foster children's success as readers (Sulzby 1991; Morrow 1991). It is ironic, then, that in many classrooms, these two practices are considered "frills" and are only included "if there's time." We need to recognize their essential role in children's growth as readers.

Field Notes: Teacher-To-Teacher

Creating a special area in the room for reading aloud is important to me. Our carpeted reading corner is a pleasant place, with students' art on the walls to create an aesthetic mood. I treat this event with seriousness and ritual; it is granted the same respect as any important ceremony in our lives. The students may sit or recline, but they must take full responsibility for "entertaining" the story that is being read. Once I have finished reading the story and closed the book, they sit up straight and position themselves for a sharing of thoughts, feelings, and illuminations about their experience during reading.

Karen Smith
Herrera Elementary School
Phoenix, Arizona

Reading aloud to young children is the number one factor associated with success in school.

Reading aloud to young children is the number one factor associated with success in school (Sulzby 1991). When our students come to school without these read-aloud experiences, instead of labeling them "disadvantaged," our role as teachers is to spend more time reading aloud to them in our classrooms. Reading aloud to young children introduces them to concepts of print, book language, and story structures, all of which differ from the oral language that surrounds them in daily life.

For children of all ages, I use read-alouds to introduce them to quality literature that they might not find on their own. As students listen to books and discuss them with classmates, they develop understandings about the structures of different kinds of books, the strategies they can use to understand what they read on their own, and a wealth of literary experiences that they can draw on in their daily lives and in other reading experiences.

When you choose books to read aloud in your classroom, avoid the high-interest books that your students are already reading on their own and consider books that will challenge them as readers. For young children, this means choosing picture books that they are not yet able to read independently. For example, they can understand and delight in the language and story as they share Sylvester's mishaps when a magical pebble turns him into a rock, in William Steig's *Sylvester and the Magic Pebble*.

They can recreate the magic of vaudeville through Karen Ackerman's *Song and Dance Man*; share stories about fear with a grandfather and grandson in Mary Stolz's *Storm* in the *Night*; and learn about honesty and hard work from a grandfather who has just arrived from Mexico in Eve Bunting's *A Day's Work*.

For older children, this may mean reading historical fiction and fantasy, not just humor and realistic fiction. Children often discover that the difficult books they reject on their own become meaningful experiences when read aloud with the support of their classroom community. In Goshen, Indiana, Kaylene Yoder Ediger discovered that her sixth graders had never explored fantasy. To introduce them to this genre, she read aloud Natalie Babbit's *Tuck Everlasting*, a realistic story with a touch of fantasy: an everyday family discovers the fountain of everlasting life. She also read Lloyd Alexander's *The Black Cauldron*, a fantasy about the fight between good and evil in an imaginary kingdom. The class discussed the story plots and structures of fantasy.

As her students learned how to read fantasy, not surprisingly, more of them began choosing this genre for their independent reading.

If your students have negative responses to reading any kind of book, then it may be best to begin read-aloud with high-interest humorous books. When I was working with a group of fourth graders who had negative attitudes toward books and read-aloud, I began with Judy Blume's books because I knew her humor would interest them. If you need specific recommendations for read-aloud titles, I recommend Jim Trelease's *The New Read-Aloud Handbook*, Eden Ross Lipson's *The New York Times Parent's Guide to the Best Books for Children*, and Judy Freeman's *Books Kids Will Sit Still For: The Complete Read-Aloud Guide*. These resources will help you make thoughtful decisions about the books you want to read aloud to push your students as readers and thinkers.

Remember that the length of a book is not necessarily related to its reading challenge. Chapter books are sometimes written in a simplistic style without a real message. Likewise, picture books can be quite complex and present issues that challenge both children and adults.

Remember that the length of a book is not necessarily related to its reading challenge.

Poetry can play an important role in read-aloud experiences if we take time to share it with children. As a teacher, I kept several good poetry anthologies, such as *Sing a Song of Popcorn* by Beatrice de Regniers, *The Random House Book of Poetry* by Jack Prelutsky, and *Knock on a Star* by X. J. Kennedy on my desk, keeping the right poem handy for the right moment to use for transitions between different parts of the day. I also paired poems with books, actually gluing the poem into the back of the book so that I could share the poem when I read that book aloud. For example, I read David McCord's poem, "Crows," whenever I read aloud the picture book *Crow Boy* by Taro Yashima.

SHOPTALK

Benedict, Susan and Lenore Carlisle, eds. *Beyond Words: Picture Books for Older Readers and Writers*. Portsmouth, New Hampshire: Heinemann, 1992.

The authors and educators in this edited book share ideas for using picture books—with readers of all ages—to encourage creativity and critical thinking.

Teachers from first grade through high school explain how they use picture books to enhance their reading and writing curriculums.

When you read poetry aloud to your students, you'll want to avoid using a sing-song voice. Your own natural intonation works best. You may also choose to purchase tapes of poets reading their own work. Because poetry is usually short and conceptually dense, I read a poem aloud several times. Then I invite children to share. I ask, "What were you thinking or seeing in your mind as you listened to this poem?" I used to ask students, "Did you like it?" but found this question did not invite discussion. Sometimes, though, we don't talk about the poem at all. We simply listen and enjoy it.

It's also important to include informational books in your read-aloud experiences. Once upon a time, informational books were dry and uninteresting. No more. Check informational authors such as Aliki, Gail Gibbons, Joanna Cole, Russell Freeman, Diane Hoyt-Goldsmith, Seymour Simon, and Ann Morris. Aliki writes many easy-to-understand picture books on intriguing topics—mummies, dinosaurs, and how books are made. Gail Gibbons creates brightly illustrated informational books for young children. Joanna Cole's innovative *Magic Schoolbus* series, with illustrator Bruce Degen, captures the attention of many children. Russell Freedman writes photo biographies and historical informational books for older students on children of the Wild West, immigrant children, and famous people, such as Abraham Lincoln and Franklin Roosevelt. Diane Hoyt-Goldsmith's profile series of American Indian children tells about their lives in today's world. Seymour Simon's many science informational books uses excellent photographs to help make scientific topics accessible to children. Ann Morris creates concept books based on photographs, with subjects such as bread and hats, to introduce young children to their multicultural world. These informational books make excellent read-alouds for any classroom.

Few doubt the benefits of reading aloud to both primary and intermediate grade children. When students listen to books read aloud, they grow as individual readers, but they also bond as members of a classroom community. Together they create a shared reading history. In my university classes, I often ask undergraduates to write about their literacy memories. Many describe unhappy times of round-robin reading and SRA cards, but these young adults also remember teachers who read aloud to them. Fresh in their minds are happy memories of sitting together with their classmates and listening to a good book. Parents and children also cherish the cozy, loving experience of reading a good book together. Reading aloud in school creates these feelings of warmth and togetherness that are so essential to nurturing learning communities where learners feel safe.

S H O P T A L K

Freeman, Evelyn and Diane Person, eds. *Using Nonfiction Trade Books in the Elementary Classroom: From Ants to Zeppelins.* Urbana, Illinois: National Council of Teachers of English, 1992.

Classroom teachers, teacher educators, librarians, and children's authors talk about the link between nonfiction and the elementary curriculum. The chapters include discussions about nonfiction as a genre, in addition to many suggestions for classroom practice and lists of informational books. Teachers will find information ranging from descriptions of specific books to classroom activities to full thematic units.

Reading books together provides a common point of reference that you and your students can use in future experiences.

Reading books together provides a common point of reference that you and your students can use in future experiences. We choose some books to read aloud simply because they are wonderful literature we want to share with children, but we choose others because they relate to issues that students are pursuing in their personal lives or through inquiry. Students are able to bring more to their understandings of the read-aloud when the books are connected to issues that matter to them. They also take new understandings from the read-aloud back to their inquiries and personal lives.

At Warren Elementary School in Tucson, sixth-grade teacher Leslie Kahn read aloud *Journey of the Sparrows,* Fran Leeper Buss's story of a family of political refugees from El Salvador and their struggle to survive. Her students were beginning a historical study of the Holocaust and she wanted to provide a modern-day context for learning about issues central to the Holocaust—separation of family, death, difficult living conditions, racism, and political oppression. *Journey of the Sparrows* helped students make strong connections to events that happened long ago. Be on the lookout for ways you can help your students make similar emotional and academic connections.

Read aloud to your students every day as often as you can. To begin the morning, read a picture book. You might then read from a chapter book or another picture book. Right after lunch, read aloud to help children regain their focus. And, right before reading or writing work time, read books related to the children as readers and writers. We read books by authors or illustrators who are being studied. In addition to being a natural fit into the current topic, these readings also help the children learn strategies that will improve their own writing. For example, when a group of third graders were interested in making their stories more mysterious, I chose Chris Van Allsburg's picture books to read aloud at the beginning of writing workshop. They noted how he often included partial views of objects in his illustrations, withheld important information until the last page, used surprise endings, and maintained the reader's suspense.

It's essential that children have a time when they can choose their reading materials and read for their own enjoyment and learning, without mandatory book reports or discussions.

Following your read-aloud with a brief class discussion will help children think more deeply about a book. At the same time, they learn how to talk about books, and interact and converse with one another. If the book is particularly powerful or enjoyable, you might encourage your students to respond through art, drama, dance, music, or writing.

If possible, display the books that you read aloud in your classroom library. These books will be in high demand by students to read on their own. Once students have heard a book read aloud and the story becomes more predictable, students find it easier to read independently. Some teachers purchase multiple copies of the longer chapter books because they know that many students will want to read these books. The impact of these read-aloud experiences then continues long past the actual in-class reading.

Wide Reading, Partner Reading, and Book Sharing

Wide reading is known by many names—SSR (sustained silent reading), DEAR (drop everything and read), and independent reading. Regardless of the name, it's essential that children have a time when they can choose their reading materials and read for their own enjoyment and learning, without mandatory book reports or discussions; they simply read for their own purposes. (Students may want to keep a list of the titles they are reading if this list has a purpose in your classroom.)

The federal government's report on reading, *Becoming a Nation of Readers* (1985), shows that time devoted to independent reading is consistently related to gains in reading proficiencies. The report notes that seventy percent of "reading time" in many classrooms is spent filling out worksheets and workbooks. Yet, there is no correlation between this work and reading achievement—the seatwork simply fills time. In giving students books to read instead of having them do worksheets, we can dramatically influence children's growth—in vocabulary, comprehension, and fluency, as well as their interest and enjoyment of literature.

The research shows that students are not getting this time to read at home or at school. A study by Anderson, Fielding, and Wilson (1988) of fifth-grade students found that they spent an average of zero to four minutes reading outside school and seven minutes reading inside school each day. Other research by Allington (1984) shows that readers who are experiencing difficulty with reading are given significantly less time to read inside school because they spend their time working on skills and worksheets. Wide reading in school is not simply a "filler" or a treat reserved only for those who have finished all their work. It is through wide reading that our children become readers.

You may worry about whether wide reading is appropriate for young children who cannot yet read print. Don Holdaway's research (1979) informs us that very young children who live in homes filled with literature spend hours looking at books and telling their own stories to go with the pictures. When they "read the pictures" they truly act as readers. Whether they are conventionally reading the print is not important. You'll want to help your students do the same in your classroom.

Also of real concern are older children whose reading experiences are so negative that they reject reading. We can provide these older readers with "real life" reading materials such as magazines, comics, and newspapers.

A classroom library, book displays, book talks, and book sharing—when a student reads a book with the support of a peer—all foster successful experiences with wide reading. These strategies work well with both younger and older readers. Accessibility is the key. I established a classroom library using the paperback book clubs and obtaining funding through grants, parent-teacher associations, and the school district textbook money. I regularly checked out books from the school and public libraries. It's important to note that a classroom library does not decrease use of the school library, but actually increases children's interest in using the school library.

Celebrate your classroom library. Be sure to put it in a central location in your room—don't tuck it away out of sight. Make it bright, light, and inviting. Optimally, your library should say to children "Come here, get cozy, and read." Accordingly, you'll want to include a wide range of reading materials—poetry, informational books, picture books, novels, magazines, newspapers, series books, and comic books. Some of these materials will be easy for children to read fluently, while others may be difficult. Children may only be able to read the captions and photographs in some books, but that's okay. They are still interacting with print and reading in important ways.

High-interest, light reading, such as magazines and mystery novels, make up part of our lives as readers. These materials enable us to read fluently while we relax. We can enjoy reading without having to think too hard. Children need these same experiences. They need to read highly predictable books that allow them to build fluency. These predictable books include the sets of "little books" for young children from publishers like Rigby and the Wright Group, and the series books such as *Babysitter Club* and *Goosebumps* that many paperback book clubs are offering to older students. While series books and little books do not support in-depth literature discussions, they do play a strong role in children's independent reading. You can balance this lighter reading with more complex literature that you read aloud or ask your students to discuss in literature circles.

Celebrate your classroom library.

I discovered the importance of reading materials which support children's reading efforts when working with a group of first graders. Early in the year, many predictable books were available in our classroom and the children soon became active readers who were seldom seen without books in their hands. In January, I had to return the predictable book sets. The children were left with the existing classroom library which contained few predictable books. To my amazement, the same group of children who had been reading anything in sight almost stopped reading. I quickly brought back ten to twenty "old favorites" a week to our classroom. Once again, the children became avid readers. They needed books that were familiar and easy for them to read and reread, as well as more challenging materials.

I also regularly set up displays of books on topics of interest to children and featured books of particular authors and illustrators. I increased children's interactions with these books when I briefly introduced two to three books each day from these displays.

Peer recommendations had an even more dramatic influence in encouraging the children's reading. Children are inclined to read books their friends enjoy and recommend, which is not really different from our experiences as adult readers. I found that by taking ten minutes for children to share with a partner, small group, or the whole class at the end of our wide reading, they became more comfortable talking with each other about their reading and read more broadly.

When I first introduced wide reading, I assumed that children would read individually and silently. Since I was teaching first grade at the time, I quickly realized my mistake. Children needed the support of reading with others and they rarely read silently. I was surprised to find the same need for partner reading with older students. While they spent more time reading alone than young children, they still enjoyed reading with a peer. Children who had experienced difficulty with reading were often reluctant to pick up a book on their own. However, if they could read with another child, they actually did more reading than when they had to read alone. Other children read together simply because they found the sharing pleasurable.

Partner reading can become an important ingredient in your classroom, particularly at the beginning of the school year. At Maldonado Elementary School in Tucson, Arizona, Gloria Kauffman (1995) found that partner reading encouraged children of all ages to read. It also enabled them to become more comfortable working with other children. On the first day of school, she asks children to find a partner and read together. Initially, children choose partners they already know and trust. After this first experience, she pulls children together and they talk about the different ways that they shared the reading: each person reading half of the book or reading every other page or chapter; one person reading refrains or a particular character's words, and the other person reading the rest of the book; each reading a different book to the other person.

Over the next several weeks, children are encouraged to read with some-one they've never had as a partner or someone of the opposite gender. This last request initially causes gasps of horror but begins to break down the cliques and stereotypes that prevent a classroom from becoming a com-munity. Kauffman emphasizes partner reading at the beginning of the year and continues to offer it as a choice throughout the year.

Kathyrn Mitchell Pierce (1995) of Glenridge Elementary School in St. Louis, Missouri, offers her primary multi-age students a related engagement called *read-around*. Individually, children choose a book they want to learn to read.

They ask different people in the class-room to read the book to them or with them, then sign their read-around sheet. Once they are con-fident in their ability to read it by themselves, they have an oppor-tunity to read the book aloud to the class or a small group.

Field Notes: Teacher-To-Teacher

Early in the year, Evan and Seth often worked together on read-arounds using simple predictable texts. They took their book and form all around our classroom and the building asking others to help them read the book. When they could read it independently, they signed up to share the book with me and then with their former kindergarten teacher or a few of her students. The end of each read-around experience was marked by placing the completed read-around form in their working file. Later, during conferences, these forms helped to provide a record of the books students had read and the amount of support necessary to be able to read a book aloud to others.

Kathryn Mitchell Pierce
Glenridge Elementary School
St. Louis, Missouri

SHOPTALK

All four of these periodicals are excellent resources for keeping up on current books, trends, and reviews in children's and adolescent literature.

Book Links is a bimonthly magazine that provides annotated bibliographies on an array of topics. It is an especially good source for locating new releases on science and social studies topics. It also contains sections on book strategies, classroom connections, the inside story of a book, and visual links.

The Bulletin of the Center for Children's Books is a monthly journal that focuses solely on critical reviews of current books for children and adolescents.

The Horn Book Magazine is a bimonthly publication with critical reviews on children's literature. It also provides articles on authors, illustrators, Caldecott and Newbery award winners, and other issues.

The New Advocate, which I edit, is published four times a year and focuses on the connections between literature and teaching. It includes inspiring and informative articles by authors and illustrators, with practical reflections on using literature in the classroom.

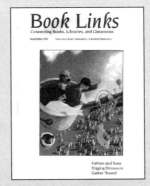

Readers Theater and Choral Reading

Readers theater and choral reading highlight oral reading for real purposes. For many years, my students read orally to prove they had read the story. Both they and I dreaded sitting in reading group with each person taking a turn reading aloud while others kept their eyes on their books, but their minds focused elsewhere. Readers theater and choral reading involve the dramatic oral interpretation of stories and poems for an audience. In readers theater, interpretation is done through the use of voice and facial expressions, so the focus is on meaning, not on pronouncing words correctly. Because of this focus, props and costumes are not used, although background music may be incorporated.

To create a readers theater, a story is divided into speaking parts. Usually those parts involve one or two narrators and the characters. Stories involving dialogue between several characters, like the *Frog and Toad* books by Arnold Lobel, are the easiest to arrange as a readers theater. Stories with rich, rhythmic language and repeating refrains, such as folktales, are also good choices.

Students choose their parts and read aloud without props or costumes. They can sit on stools or stand in designated spots to read their parts. Students may also turn away from the audience when they are not reading or if their character is not involved in the action.

After one group has presented, start a class discussion about that group's interpretation and talk about other ways they might arrange the script or change their oral interpretation. It's both fun and exciting to give another reading of the same story—either the original group can read again or another group can try a new reading. You and your students will enjoy the dialogue and critical thinking that repeat performances inspire.

Readers theater helps readers learn that any story is open to many different interpretations. There is no one way to read a story, and the different readings allow students to discuss what makes some interpretations more convincing.

Readers theater is accessible to readers of various proficiencies. When they read orally, children are often eager to take risks because they enjoy the performance. In a summer reading program, I was pleasantly surprised to see children who were labeled "poor" readers give the adults the shorter parts while they kept the more involved parts for themselves. Because they practiced before presenting the script, they felt comfortable taking risks and were successful. Once children have had a number of experiences with readers theater scripts, they can create their own or continue using books. The prepared scripts become part of the classroom library and one of the options children can choose during wide reading. The scripts can also be used to read informally with others.

Readers theater helps readers learn that any story is open to many different interpretations.

Choral reading involves oral interpretation of poetry. Leslie Kahn and I introduced choral reading to her sixth graders at Warren Elementary School in Tucson, Arizona. We gave them the well-known nursery rhyme, "Hickory Dickory Dock," and invited them to try out as many different arrangements as possible. We then talked about the ways we had found to vary the combinations of speaking arrangements, voice quality, and movements, and discussed other possibilities as well.

Speaking Arrangements
- unison—everyone reading at the same time
- refrains—whole group reads together on refrains
- line-a-child or line-a-group
- antiphonal—two groups who go back and forth
- cumulative—adding more and more voices on each line or stanza
- rounds—two to three groups with each group starting to read one line or stanza behind the others

Voice Quality
- loudness or softness
- the smoothness—reading in a flowing or staccato voice
- speed
- placement of pauses

• emphasis on particular words

• different tones or pitches in dialogue

Adding chants or body movements while another group chorally reads the poem or rhyme is also a good variation.

In New York City, Shelley Harwayne (1993) gave small groups of students fifteen minutes every day to create arrangements for the same poem. Each group presented their interpretation to the class. Afterward, the class briefly spoke about which presentations they had found most effective. Throughout the rest of the year, students were invited to select poetry for choral reading. This engagement increased students' enjoyment of poetry and helped them develop effective strategies for oral reading.

Learning about language enables readers to actively reflect on their knowledge about language, literature, and the reading process.

```
D I A L O G U E

How do I help my students learn language in my classroom?

_____

_____

How can I make my practices even more effective?

_____

_____

What other engagements with learning language do I want to add
to my curriculum?

_____

_____
```

Students naturally learn language when they read literature. However, they also need to look at language itself—to develop their reading strategies and increase their awareness about the structures of stories and books. Reflecting on their reading helps students in developing a repertoire of strategies that support them as proficient and flexible readers and writers.

Engagements for Learning about Language

Learning about language enables readers to actively reflect on their knowledge about language, literature, and the reading process. As students become aware of how language functions, they take control of their own learning and grow as readers. As Carolyn Burke says, "a little awareness goes a long way," so we need to devote only a small part of the children's total reading time to this learning.

After reading and considering the meaning of a book, students might engage in a strategy lesson on the use of context clues or a particular story structure. For example, a group of third graders laughed their way through Arnold Lobel's *Fables* and later returned to the book to figure out the story structure of a fable. As part of an ocean unit, I read aloud a book about ocean animals to a group of first graders. After talking about what they had learned, we went back to the book to see how they could use context clues to identify a particular animal before it was named in the text. Meaningful uses of literature naturally lead to learning about language. In turn, readers have a purpose and context for exploring how literature works.

Children learn about written language through author studies, shared and guided reading, and strategy lessons. These engagements build from experiences where students read whole texts for real purposes. They are not isolated skill activities, but responses to the needs of readers. The engagements require a classroom where students read widely, and where teachers and students are continually involved in evaluation to identify students' needs and strengths.

Reading To Understand Written Language

Children's books often include characters who read and write. When teachers and children read and discuss these books, Yetta Goodman (1988) suggests they consider the nature of literacy and its functions and purposes for society. Indeed, literacy is an important way of learning—inside and outside of school. To that end, the following lists will help you find books about celebrating various functions of literacy, such as

personal journals, written correspondence, stories, and the joys of reading and writing

I'm in Charge of Celebrations by Byrd Baylor

Penny Pollard's Diary by Robin Klein

The Jolly Postman by Janet and Allan Ahlberg

Your Best Friend, Kate by Pat Brisson

Angel Child, Dragon Child by Michele Surat

Cherries and Cherry Pits by Vera Williams

Good Books, Good Times (poetry) compiled by Lee Bennett Hopkins

Hey World, Here I Am! (poetry and short stories) by Jean Little

children playing name games and learning to write their names

The Day of Ahmed's Secret by Florence Heide

Mary Wore Her Red Dress and Henry Wore His Green Sneakers by Merle Peek

children and adults learning to read

The Wednesday Surprise by Eve Bunting

Mrs. Dunphy's Dog by Catharine O'Neill

Reading by Jan Ormerod

Papa's Stories by Delores Johnson

If You Were a Writer by Jean Lowery Nixon

Just Call Me Stupid by Tom Birdseye

Amber on the Mountain by Tony Johnston

Bee Tree by Patricia Polacco

Aunt Chip and the Great Triple Creek Dam Affair by Patricia Polacco

and youngsters learning to read through the use of environmental print.

When Will I Read? by Miriam Cohen

Signs by Ron and Nancy Goor

I Read Signs by Tana Hoban

I Walk and Read by Tana Hoban

The Tale of Thomas Mead by Pat Hutchins

The Signmaker's Assistant by Tedd Arnold

Speaking of learning to read through the use of environmental print, I take young ones on walks around the school and the local neighborhood to find signs they can read. Children draw pictures of what they can read or take snapshots of signs with an instant camera on our environmental print walks. We collect the pictures in a group-composed book. Sometimes, I invite children to bring printed material of all sorts from home—cereal boxes, toothpaste containers, soup cans, even magazine and newspaper ads—to make their own "I Can Read" books. These fun learning engagements are wonderfully effective in expanding the children's experiences with signs and labels. From these learning engagements and the various books that involve literacy, children can see that reading is not just something that occurs in school. It is an important part of literate people's lives.

Author Studies

Sometimes young children believe that machines or "perfect" adults write the books they read. That's why author studies are a wonderful way to bring to life the authors behind the books children love. When engaging in author studies, children hear about the lives of favorite authors and illustrators. They also learn about their writing and illustrating strategies and look at connections among their books. When authors become "real," children are more likely to critique the books they read. When they visit the library, instead of feeling overwhelmed by the volume of books, children can look for books by authors and illustrators who have become their friends. And, once children are familiar with an author's work, they more easily comprehend other books by that author. Author studies also expand choices, giving students the opportunity to learn about strategies that they can use in their reading, writing, and illustrating.

As children participate in an author study, they naturally engage in talk about an author's language and writing style. In a study of William Steig's books, second graders talked about his use of words that they'd never heard before, but could understand within the context of the story. First graders reveled in the repetition of Eric Carle's books and noted the way his pictures help to tell the story. In both cases, I built on children's observations in introducing reading strategies related to context clues, story and language patterns, and picture clues.

Sixth graders examined Eric Carle's work to explore book formats and designs that they could use in their own publishing. A group of fifth graders were intrigued to discover that Patricia MacLachlan begins her writing with a character instead of a plot. These young authors then started to focus more on characterization in their writing.

Each morning in my classroom, I read aloud a book by the author we were featuring that week. On the first day of our study, I told children a bit about the author's life and introduced a display of the author's books. On the following days, I read from the author's books, reading aloud picture books or excerpts from longer chapter books. I continued to share anecdotes from the author's life. Often, our study would lead us into drama, art, music, and writing projects.

I also made it a point to identify the author's and illustrator's names of every book we read together in the classroom. I found that reading the book jacket information to children was a quick, easy way to introduce them to authors.

Sandy Kaser and her fifth-grade students began a study of Jane Yolen after encountering some of her books in a theme unit on birds of prey. They went to several libraries and gathered every book they could find to create a display of her work. They spent many hours happily browsing and reading her books and then dividing them into different sets according to topic and genre. The students put these text sets to work for themselves in wide reading and literature circles. As they discussed the books and listened to Kaser read aloud from other Yolen books, students created a chart that visually marked the characteristics of Yolen's books—her writing style, the topics of her books, and the kinds of characters she creates.

Because Yolen's books cover so many different topics and range from picture books to complex novels, students were able to find books that matched their interests and reading proficiencies. They created posters to "sell" their favorite books, and also developed exhibits, displaying these projects throughout the school and in the school library. During these experiences, Kaser shared excerpts from articles that Yolen had written about her work. The author's comments about her writing techniques inspired them to explore new strategies for writing from their own experiences.

Children may also research their favorite authors. They can do this individually or in a literature circle with other students who share their interest in an author. The best source for information about authors is a large encyclopedia called *Something about the Author*. New volumes are added each year. Other quality sources are *How Writers Write* by Pamela Lloyd, and *Talking with Artists* and *Talking with Artists, Volume II* by Pat Cummings.

Children may want to write to their favorite authors, but those letters should grow out of their desire to communicate with that person. Letters to an author lose their meaning when they are teacher-assigned.

Of course, children are thrilled when an author actually comes to their school. The author may be well-known or a local person publishing through a small press. If an author does visit, be sure your children have already read and responded to the author's books. To assure a lively, productive visit, ask your students to consider what they want to discuss before the visit.

Shared and Guided Reading

Shared and guided reading provide maximum support for readers. Inviting your most hesitant readers to read and reread familiar predictable materials with others can ease them into successful and enjoyable reading. As children begin to read, they are supported and encouraged to take risks and make predictions based on sentence structure and meaning.

Shared reading usually refers to whole group engagements where the teacher and class read together in unison or through choral reading from Big Books and other highly predictable materials. Guided reading refers to these same experiences in a small group setting. While there are many variations of shared and guided reading, all are based on readers supporting each other using a predictable text.

The books, poetry, rhymes, and songs used for shared and guided reading are predictable in several ways. Although predictable books are usually associated with young children, predictability can be a characteristic of books for all age levels. Books become predictable when they reflect children's own life experiences. Children who've grown up near the ocean relate to stories about ocean life more than books about the desert. Books also become predictable when children encounter them repeatedly. They can more easily read books they've already heard read aloud at school or home or seen on television or at the movies. Some children read many books of the same type, such

Inviting your most hesitant readers to read and reread familiar predictable materials with others can ease them into successful and enjoyable reading.

as mysteries or science fiction. Accordingly, these too become predictable. Children can also find books by the same author, in the same genre, or from a particular series to be predictable.

Lynn Rhodes (1981) examined the predictable books used with young children and found several elements that characterized predictability. These include

- repetitive patterns or refrains
- the match between text and illustration
- the rhythm of the language
- familiar sequences (numbers, days)
- rhymes and cumulative patterns.

Bill Martin Jr.'s *Brown Bear, Brown Bear* and Eric Carle's *The Very Hungry Caterpillar* are two books that use these organizational devices. *The Very Hungry Caterpillar*, for example, uses the predictable sequence of the days of the week and numbers, supportive pictures, and the refrain, "But he was still hungry." Familiar folktale versions of "The Gingerbread Boy" and "The House That Jack Built" use cumulative patterns where each new page adds phrases to the increasing repetition of the details from previous pages. For older children, series books, such as the popular *Babysitter Club* and *Goosebumps* can provide smooth transitions into chapter books since each book is based around similar characters and basic plot structures.

In these learning engagements, the teacher usually reads a predictable book to an entire class or small group of young children. Then, the children join in on the reading. When I read aloud *The Very Hungry Caterpillar* to a group of first graders, I first showed them the cover of the book and read the title to them so they could make predictions about the story. I then read the story, inviting them to join in on the refrain "but he was still hungry" whenever they felt ready. At various points, I stopped and had them predict what the next word or phrase would be or what they thought would happen on the next page. Most of the children were reading the predictable refrain by the end of the first reading.

From *The Very Hungry Caterpillar*, reprinted by permission of Philomel Books.

Responding enthusiastically to the story, the children were eager to hear it again. On the second reading, many more children joined in on the repetitive sections and I often quieted my voice so they were reading parts alone. The unison rereading provided support for all the readers—for children who were able to easily read the print to children who followed the group's lead but could not read the print on their own. Everyone joined in as they were able.

After this second reading of the book, I encouraged students to share their connections to the story. They talked about their favorite foods and their experiences with caterpillars and butterflies. We also talked about their favorite parts of the story and whether their predictions matched the story.

We read Carle's story several more times over the next week, and each time, more children were able to read with the rest of the group. The rereadings allowed children to become familiar with the book's story structure, gain fluency in oral reading, begin to notice certain visual features, and become comfortable with the language.

The Very Hungry Caterpillar became a class favorite and was especially useful in sparking explorations about the story's language. For example, children found words and phrases they could read on each page. Another time, they looked through the book to find words that began with a certain letter. The needs of your students will determine what aspects of language you'll choose to highlight in a particular book.

I wrote the parts of the story on cardboard strips and children used these strips in a variety of ways. Some matched the strips with the Big Book. Others used the strips on their own to reconstruct the story. Still others worked with the strips to retell the story using a sock puppet and felt cutouts of the fruits. Through these experiences, children became more familiar with the structure of the story and the language patterns.

The tadpole turns into a frog!

Next, I invited small groups of students to create their own versions of the story. One small group changed the kinds of foods the caterpillar ate. Another wrote their own book using these patterns, but changed the animal to a tadpole who eventually becomes a frog, and one group created a delightful book about an out-of-shape person who exercises and becomes fit and healthy. You'll discover that there's no end to the pattern substitutions children can create.

Field Notes: Teacher-To-Teacher

Knowing stories in common is an important component for building a group history. In our classrom, a small collection of books has evolved that we treat as members of the classroom community. Our kindergarten consults these books on a regular basis. These stories come up so frequently in our talk, inquiries, and activities that we keep them in a basket by the reading chair for quick reference.

Linda Bowers Sheppard
Arizona Public Schools
Phoenix, Arizona

Because of children's continuing interest in this story, we began an author study of Eric Carle's books and later used it for literature circle discussions. I also collected other books about caterpillars and butterflies and put them in our library corner for wide reading.

Shared reading sessions usually last about thirty minutes and begin with rereading old favorites that the children select. You'll want to move on to new stories, songs, and poems. In whole class shared reading experiences, you may want to use Big Books that have enlarged print so all children can see both the print and the illustrations. You can purchase commercial Big Books, but creating Big Books is a fun and worthwhile class project; children draw the illustrations and you or an adult helper can write the text. You can showcase songs, poems, and rhymes by placing them on large charts. In small group guided reading, every student usually has a copy of the predictable book which means you'll need multiple copies of each predictable title.

SHOPTALK

Holdaway, Don. *The Foundations of Literacy*. Portsmouth, New Hampshire: Heinemann, 1979.

Based on his years of research and work in New Zealand classrooms, Holdaway writes of learning to read from a developmental perspective. He describes the theoretical framework for his model of early literacy and gives practical suggestions for ways to use Big Books and shared reading in the classroom.

Slaughter, Judith Pollard. *Beyond Storybooks: Young Children and the Shared Book Experience*. Newark, Delaware: International Reading Association, 1993.

If you are interested in learning more about implementing highly predictable reading materials in your curriculum, this practical book is for you. Topics covered include making your own Big Books, organizing shared reading and writing experiences, creating learning activities based on books, and developing thematic units around predictable books. It also provides a bibliography of predictable books.

In the classroom, in addition to group reading and rereading, we need independent exploration time to help children gain understanding of a particular story.

Shared and guided reading are based on Don Holdaway's (1979) observations of young children who learned to read easily and naturally by looking at books while sitting on their parents' laps. They heard the same books read time and again and spent many hours of playtime experimenting with the books on their own. In the classroom, in addition to group reading and rereading, we need independent exploration time to help children gain understanding of a particular story. These predictable stories should be displayed in the classroom library so that students—especially those who need more support and repetition—can continue to read these books on their own.

Teaching for Reading Strategies

Strategy lessons, or reading conferences, enable students to reflect on themselves as readers. Regardless of the name, these curricular engagements all help students focus on cognitive and social strategies necessary for becoming more proficient readers.

Strategy lessons allow students to participate in a reading experience that highlights a particular strategy, such as prediction or self-monitoring, and to reflect on its use in their own reading. For example, I used "Synonym Substitution" (Goodman, Watson and Burke 1996) with a group of third graders who were having difficulty reading unfamiliar terms; the students were overemphasizing letter-sound relationships to the exclusion of meaning and syntax cues. This strategy lesson encouraged them to substitute a word they didn't recognize with a synonym they did know.

I gave students a version of the familiar story, "The Three Pigs," in which a number of words were underlined. Working in pairs, students used context clues to come up with synonyms for the underlined words or phrases and then shared their substitutions as a class or small group. I read the story aloud, stopping at underlined words, and students called out their substitutions. When I read the line, "Along came a big bad wolf," I stopped at the word "bad" and students called out synonyms, such as "awful, wrong, evil, not nice, young, and naughty." We went back and talked about why some of these synonyms did and did not work within the context of the story. The students also reflected on how and when they might use this strategy as readers.

In working with a group of fourth graders, I realized they were having difficulty comprehending mystery stories—they did not understand how these books were organized and how authors of mysteries provide clues for readers. I chose *From the Mixed-Up Files of Mrs. Basil E. Frankweiler* by E. L. Konigsburg, as the read-aloud chapter book. As I read this book aloud to students, we discussed the kinds of connections and meanings children were finding. We talked about how the book was organized and kept a chart of the clues in the book. After we finished the book, children met in literature circles to read and discuss their own choices of mystery stories. We met as a class several times a week to talk about their strategies for reading these books. At the end of the literature circles, we created a class chart called "Strategies for Reading Mystery Books." I kept it posted on the classroom wall, and students used it as reference.

Teaching for strategies sometimes happens in a conference with an individual child. One day in October, during wide reading, I was partner reading with Erin, a struggling young reader. I suggested that she try the strategy of skipping a word and reading on to see if she could figure out the meaning. In May, when I interviewed children about their changes as readers during the year, Erin told me that learning to "read on" was a major turning point for her as a reader.

In reading with individual children or small groups, once we reach the end of the story, I find it helpful to ask them to find a place where they either accomplished some good reading work or experienced difficulty (Short 1991). If they choose a page where they struggled with figuring out a word or phrase, I ask them what strategies they tried and what else they might have done. If appropriate, I then offer an additional strategy that they might use. These brief, effective interactions encourage children to think through their current reading strategies and develop new ones.

DIALOGUE

How do I help my students learn about language in my classroom?

_____

_____

How can I make these engagements even more effective?

_____

_____

What other engagements with learning about language do I want to add to my curriculum?

_____

_____

Engagements that highlight learning about language support students in building a repertoire of reading strategies. These engagements also create an awareness of how language and stories function. Students learn to use their knowledge of language and story more efficiently and effectively to make predictions and construct meaning as they read.

Chapter 4

Learning through Language

Engagements that highlight learning through language provide the *reason* for reading—to learn about life, not to practice reading. Our emphasis is on what we are learning, not on our reading process. This chapter focuses on experiences in which students thoughtfully read books to consider meaning that is significant to them.

The extensive engagements in Chapter 3 support readers in gaining reading strategies and becoming proficient readers. The intensive engagements in this chapter support readers in becoming literate thinkers who deeply and critically consider what they read. We will look at

- theme studies
- research
- inquiry groups
- literature circles
- response to literature through art, writing, and drama.

When students read to learn about themselves and their world, they come to think critically about what they read. They consider the meanings they're creating from the written page and compare those meanings to their own experiences, other literature, and other sources of information. Literature links them to learning.

Read Your Way into Themes and Inquiry

Literature is a potentially powerful tool when your class explores new themes or inquiries. As you begin a new focus, gather fiction and nonfiction books related to the theme, and give your students time to browse and read them. They'll become familiar with the various topics related to the theme and discover added questions or issues they may want to research further.

When I worked with first graders on their family studies, I read aloud picture books that dealt with the struggles and love that exists within families. Children told many stories about their own grandparents after listening to *Now One Foot, Now the Other*, Tomie de Paola's poignant story of a young boy's relationship with his grandfather who has suffered a stroke. The first graders were also inspired by the story of a young girl's imaginary flight with her grandmother in *Abuela* by Arthur Dorros. Barbara Hazen's *Tight Times* helped them understand the difficulties in some families when a father loses his job, and they empathized with the grandmother, mother, and daughter in Vera Williams' *A Chair for My Mother* when a fire destroys the characters belongings. They shared their own family stories after listening to a mother tell her daughter stories in *Tell Me a Story, Mama* by Angela Johnson.

Field Notes: Teacher-To-Teacher

I talk to my students at the beginning of each year about "entertaining" a text the same way they entertain guests in their homes. We reflect on the dynamics of this process and talk about how we often share advice, sympathy, and laughter with our guests. We also talk about how important it is to listen to our guests and to try to think the way they do. We realize that it is often through interactions with others that we are able to create meaning in and about our own lives. I stress that we need to meet and treat book characters the same as we do guests.

Karen Smith
Herrera Elementary School
Phoenix, Arizona

I also collected a families theme set of fiction, nonfiction, and poetry that the children could explore during wide reading. While we discussed these books, I took careful notes of the inquiries and the connections the children were making. Many of the youngsters' remarks pertained to family problems and the various roles that grandparents played in their lives. Instead of deciding ahead of time what topics and issues we would study, I let the children's comments guide the direction of our family inquiries. Their issues involved relationships with grandparents, adjustments in families due to divorce and new babies, parents' lack of understanding about "kid stuff," and sibling fighting.

In Tucson, Leslie Kahn became concerned about the racism that her fifth-grade students accepted as a natural part of their community. She decided to introduce an inquiry cycle on the Holocaust (Kahn 1994). Although her students had never heard of the Holocaust, Kahn believed that as they studied racism in the context of Nazi Germany, they could more effectively recognize and critique racism in their school and community. She read aloud Fran Leeper Buss's story of illegal immigrants, *Journey of the Sparrows*, to introduce issues of political oppression and racism in our society.

Instead of deciding ahead of time what topics and issues we would study, I let the children's comments guide the direction of our family inquiries.

Responding to her students' fascination with facts about weapons and methods of death during the Holocaust, Kahn brought in a variety of nonfiction. She was not content, however, to let her students focus solely on facts about death, particularly given some of their gang participation. To that end, she read aloud from thought-provoking picture books to encourage them to consider human suffering, injustice, and prejudice. Two books set in concentration camps particularly touched students. In *Rose Blanche* by Roberto Innocenti, a young German girl discovers a concentration camp and sneaks food to starving children at the risk of her own life. *Let the Celebrations Begin* by Margaret Wild is set in a camp near the end of the war while emaciated people prepare a celebration—even though some of the victims despair of ever being liberated.

Kahn filled the classroom with novels, information books, picture books, and primary source information such as newspapers and eyewitness accounts. Students dramatized some of the experiences they read about (Kahn, Fisher and Pitt 1994). They also interviewed Holocaust survivors who visited their classroom. In addition, students participated in literature circles with novels that had Holocaust themes. These included *Snow Treasure* by Marie McSwigan, *The Upstairs Room* by Johanna Reiss, *Number the Stars* by Lois Lowry, *Summer of My German Soldier* by Bette Greene, and *Escape from*

Warsaw by Ian Serraillier. Kahn encouraged students to record their impressions in learning logs as they read, browsed, and talked with others. The literature circle discussions helped students make decisions about topics they wanted to pursue through inquiry groups.

Field Notes: Teacher-To-Teacher

Today we read *An Angel for Solomon Singer*, a picture book by Cynthia Rylant about a lonely man living in New York City who finds companionship and his dreams in a cafe. The kids really picked up on the idea that dreams and friendship can keep an individual afloat when times are hard. They related this concept to the Holocaust by noting that dreams and hope were essential to the survival of many people in the concentration camps.

Leslie Kahn
Robins Elementary School
Tucson, Arizona

Literature Supports Research

As children explore a topic, their questions become more focused. With your guidance, they realize they can systematically investigate those questions through further research. Whether literature plays a major role in their research depends on the issues they are pursuing.

In the first-grade family study, I created text sets of picture books around the topics that the children raised. These sets consisted of five to ten related books on topics such as grandparents, divorce, new babies, sibling rivalry, and getting along with parents. The books were available for students to explore during our wide reading. Each day I read aloud several books from a set and we discussed the issues these books raised for children and the connections to their personal experiences. Sometimes, students first met as partners to discuss the book I had read aloud. Then, they came back to the whole group to talk about their connections and personal experiences related to the book.

From class discussions that grew out of the first-grade family study I described, the children became interested in "remember when" family stories (Short and Harste 1996). To collect these oral stories, the children interviewed family members and shared the stories each morning during our opening class meeting. They told stories about getting lost, accidents and broken bones, special trips, family events, and embarrassing situations. They later wrote some of these stories during writing workshop time and published them. In addition, we formed small group literature circles to discuss picture books by Pat Hutchins, such as *Tom and Sam* and *Titch*, in which she writes about her own family.

Sometimes the role of literature in children's inquiries changes. Let's return to the Holocaust study that Leslie Kahn's fifth-grade class did. Her students made extensive use of literature in their early investigations. But once they finished their literature circles on Holocaust novels and moved into systematic research, other sources were more important. I mentioned that many of their questions related to racism and gangs in their own community. Accordingly, their research primarily consisted of interviews, field notes, and surveys. However, along with their field research, some of the students continued to use books as reference sources.

Literature is a tool that supports children's investigations of a topic or question. Only as the focus of the inquiry becomes clear can decisions be made about how literature might or might not play into their inquiry. When I used to plan my theme units, I gathered my favorite books and supporting activities. But I found that children were spending too much time reading about topics and were not actively *doing* history and science. When I work with teachers, we fill the room with materials, literature, and observation centers. We listen carefully to children's interests and questions, and then determine how literature might support their inquiries (Short, Schroeder, Laird, Kauffman, Ferguson and Crawford 1996).

Field Notes: Teacher-To-Teacher

The students are now very involved in their inquiry projects. Several kids are learning about Hitler and the entire class is fascinated with the Holocaust. Other children are studying a variety of issues, including concentration camps, the types of planes used in World War II, the atomic bomb, nutrition and starvation, art created during the Holocaust, and how children played in the ghetto and the camps. Derrick's topic is particularly pertinent and interesting. He is comparing Nazi youth groups with today's gangs.

Leslie Kahn
Robins Elementary School
Tucson, Arizona

Children should enter the story world of fiction and nonfiction to learn about life and make sense of their world, not to answer a series of questions.

Literature Circles

Reading is a transactional process. In *The Reader, the Text, and the Poem*, Louise Rosenblatt argues that readers construct understandings by bringing meaning *to* as well as taking meaning *from* a text. Children should enter the story world of fiction and nonfiction to learn about life and make sense of their world, not to answer a series of questions. They bring their tentative understandings of these books to literature circles where they share their experiences with each other. While they share, they critique their interpretations and connections. Listen to what Gloria Kauffman's nine-year-old student Chris had to say.

> Everyone has a chance to give their opinion and even if you don't agree with that person, you keep on talking because you know that you will get more ideas. You aren't trying to figure out one right answer. In reading groups, when someone gave the right answer, we were done talking. In literature circles, we keep on going. We try to come up with as many different directions as possible.

Ken Mochizuki's *Baseball Saved Us* became the focus of a discussion on human rights in Gloria Kauffman's fifth-grade classroom. The students identified with this story of a young Japanese American boy in a World War II internment camp who plays baseball to deal with prejudice. Ruben, Ramon, Tino, Rudy, and John talked about their own experiences playing baseball and nervously trying to please their fathers. They also discussed instances of racism in their own school and connected the story to Jane Yolen's *The Devil's Arithmetic* and to concentration camps. In addition, they made connections to slavery, an issue they had dealt with in an earlier study. Through these connections, they were able to deeply examine racism and self-identity within the book and also within their own lives.

Literature circles offer readers the opportunity to become literate. The discussions that evolve in these circles support readers in becoming critical thinkers. Although dialogue lies at the heart of all literature circles, there is no "right" way to integrate the circles into the curriculum. Both teachers and students make different decisions that influence the focus of the groups (Hanssen 1990).

Getting Started

The number of students in a literature circle creates different dynamics and opportunities for talk. Some teachers have their students read the same book and the whole class brainstorms important issues relating to the reading. The students then examine these issues in smaller groups, and later share their discussions individually with the class. Whole group discussions open up different perspectives and most students quickly learn how to talk about a book.

However, whole class groups often mean that fewer voices are heard, and students have no choice in the selection of literature. That's why literature circles are most often associated with small groups of four to five students, although some teachers prefer groups of six to seven (Hanssen 1990). In contrast to the whole class groups, the small groups give students a choice in the literature and more opportunities to talk with each other in a supportive context. When the small groups share, students often become interested in reading the books of the other groups.

I found that younger children require smaller groups to maintain a discussion. I have a vivid memory of sitting in a literature circle with a group of seven first graders that quickly split into two groups—of four and three children—despite my best efforts to keep everyone together. Young children have difficulty keeping their attention and waiting for their turn to talk. They are certain they will forget what they want to say if they have to wait too long. A group of four gives these students a chance to share more readily and keeps their attention focused. On the other hand, older students may find a slightly larger group more exciting because they are able to consider a wider range of ideas.

Another option is to read and discuss with a partner. These interactions are more intense because there are only two people. Barring any sidetracked discussions, both students must actively participate. The drawback, of course, is that the readers share just two perspectives. For students who have not experienced small groups, discussing with a partner is a comfortable way to begin. The partners learn how to interact with one another and take an active role in talking and listening. As always, you'll need to help students get used to the process of asking questions and discussing their thoughts.

Say Something. *Say Something* is one of my favorite ways to introduce literature circles (Short and Harste 1996). Everyone in the class pairs up to read the same story or book. One student reads aloud several paragraphs of the story to the other and stops. At that point, both students "say something" about the story—a connection, question, prediction, or comment. Taking turns, the partners continue this process until they have finished the story. Afterward, the students gather as a class to talk about it. In this way, students actively think about the story as they read and become more comfortable with the process of talking about a book.

Written Conversation. Another good partner engagement is *Written Conversation* (Short and Harste 1996). Sharing a piece of paper and a pencil, two children converse about a book through writing. This strategy encourages children to listen to each other before responding, something that is often difficult for them in oral conversations. Typically, no talking is allowed, except with younger children who often need to read their writing to each other. Please see the written conversation between two nine-year-old students in Gloria Kauffman's classroom on page 67.

Materials for Literature Circle
Shared book sets. Reading shared book sets—multiple copies of several titles (Smith 1990; Watson and Davis 1988)—is a strategy that naturally lends itself to literature circles. Leslie Kahn made use of shared book sets during the Holocaust focus, supplying multiple copies of *Snow Treasure* by Marie McSwigan, *Number the Stars* by Lois Lowry, and *Escape from Warsaw* by Ian Serraillier. Students signed up for the book and group of their choice. Because of the shared experience of reading the same book, the groups were able to have in-depth discussions of their responses to the book and their understandings of literary elements such as theme and character.

Melinda and Tommy
did you like Amelia's
Road? a little bite I
Like When Amelia's fond
the Road. I didn't like it.
Wath parkt did you
like? when she left. how
come you liked When
she left. I did
not like When she
left. Maybe I don't like what
you like do you like the
Gake K-Pot tree? its
a pretty cool book. Amelia's
Road chnts to me
Because I foned
a Place Were I
Like to go to
after school. Do
you? No. Do you
Wish that you
did? not Relly Woth
did you like in
the Great Kupok tree?
when the snake Talked to
him. So did I
but my bust Part
Was When all
the amelas tode
hem not to jipe
down the Great
kapok Tree.

Text sets. Collecting sets of multiple copies of literature takes time. That's why I have found text sets so useful, since they're related books with a single copy of each title (Short 1992). In each group, students read different books, share their books with each other, and search for connections among these books. The books in a set are closely related in some way—theme, topic, author, illustrator, genre, or culture. Usually the sets contain literature from a variety of genres and provide readers with different perspectives on the same theme or topic.

In a fifth-grade focus on family, Sandy Kaser put together text sets of picture books and poetry on fathers, mothers, brothers and sisters, grandparents, and family stories. Her students at Warren Elementary School in Tucson chose one set of these books to discuss. The grandparent set had books such as *Knots on a Counting Rope* by Bill Martin Jr. and John Archambault, *Grandma's Joy* by Eloise Greenfield, *The Always Prayer Shawl* by Sheldon Oberman, *A Birthday Basket for Tia* by Pat Mora, and *Poems for Grandmothers* collected by Myra Cohn Livingston. This set of culturally diverse books focused on the stories and traditions passed between grandparents and grandchildren.

When I began using text sets with children, I soon realized that students engaged in a unique type of discussion with these sets. While shared book conversations involve an intensive study of one book, text set discussions include more retellings and a look at broad connections and comparisons across literature. Readers see literature as part of a larger connected whole and become aware of diverse perspectives on similar topics.

Paired books. Knowing that text set discussions might overwhelm readers at first, I also used paired books. Two books are paired together because they offer contrasting perspectives. Paired books give students a chance to have an in-depth experience with two books while still considering connections across literature.

As part of a focus on modern culture, I created several paired book sets. I paired *Snow White in New York* by Fionna French with *Snow White* by Paul Heins, *Ruby* by Michael Emberely with *Little Red Riding Hood* by Trina Schart Hyman, and *Tucker Pfeffercorn* by Barry Moser with *Rumpelstiltskin* by Paul Galdone. Each of these paired books involve a traditional folktale set long ago and a modern variant of that tale set in today's society. Two children paired up to read and discuss one of the books. Then they met with the two children who had read and discussed the other book in their set. All four chatted together, comparing the similarities and differences between the two books.

Sharing groups. Another type of literature circle is sharing groups, where readers assemble a range of unrelated books they're exploring during their own independent reading. Because the books are unrelated to each other, the talk in these groups stays at the level of sharing, rather than moving into dialogue. These groups help students feel more comfortable talking with each other and encourages them to broaden their reading selections through peer recommendations.

Sharing groups are also appropriate when the books do not have enough depth to support an intense discussion. I experienced this when meeting with fourth-grade students who had read a popular book about Frankenstein. While they had a great deal to share, the book's emphasis on plot over theme did not provide them with issues or themes they could take further into dialogue. Initially, the classroom teacher was upset, feeling that her students were unable to sustain a quality discussion. However, when she examined the book more closely, she realized that the book itself was the problem. In trying to interest her students, she had not considered that books for literature circles need to have layers of meaning. Similarly, this lack of depth is the reason why predictable books such as Bill Martin Jr.'s *Brown Bear, Brown Bear* provide wonderful shared reading experiences for young children, but do not support discussion in literature circles.

Choosing Books for Literature Circles

Choosing the reading materials for literature circles can seem overwhelming at first. I used to worry about making poor choices. However, I found that as long as the material is meaty, well-written, and lends itself to conversation and analysis, my choices are almost unlimited—fiction and nonfiction, picture books, short stories, chapter books, and literature from different genres, including poetry and folklore. In addition, I looked through basal readers and content area textbooks for quality literature and excerpts, and used tapes of storytellers to include stories drawn from oral traditions. Other sources that I used were magazine and newspaper articles, maps, pamphlets, and children's own published stories. Children also loved nonprint texts like audio- and videotapes of music or dance, art prints, sculpture, and other hands-on artifacts.

If you have second language learners in your class, see if you can find materials written in their first languages. This way, you can avoid separating students by language. When text sets are multilingual, students can read in their first language and still participate with other language users.

As you choose the literature and other materials to work with your students, you need to consider several factors—curricular goals, student interests, and the availability of materials. Your overarching goal, however, is to choose literature that creates powerful story worlds alive with issues and connections that inspire your students to talk, analyze, and wonder.

Initiating Literature Circles

Either you or your students can give book talks to introduce the chosen literature. I found it helpful to have more books than there are groups so that all groups truly feel that they have a choice. Students have the opportunity to browse through the books for a day or two to decide which are most appealing. You can use the ones that are not chosen as class read-alouds.

Second graders taught me the importance of browsing. No sooner had I introduced them to the books for literature circles then they immediately chose the one they wanted to read and discuss. Twenty minutes later, however, they asked to switch groups. I realized that many of them had chosen the book they wanted to read, which wasn't necessarily the book they wanted to discuss. Browsing makes it easier for children to make a more informed and careful decisions.

When students are ready to choose their groups, some teachers post a sign-up sheet that lists the shared book sets or text sets with five slots for names under each title. Students sign up on a "first come, first served" basis. Other teachers have students complete a ballot with their first, second, and third choices, then the teacher makes the final group selections. You may want to experiment with different methods for forming groups. Ultimately, you'll want to stick with the method that works best for you and your students. But don't eliminate choice—choice fosters ownership and ownership helps guarantee that students will engage in the discussion.

In my work with literature circles, students choose a different circle each time based on the book they want to read. The circles relate to broad themes that we are exploring in the classroom. This way, students can bring many connections to their reading experiences. Lucy Calkins has fostered choice by having students form book clubs that stay together for several months. As each group finishes reading and discussing a book, they select the next book they want to read together. The shared context of books that are built together as a community facilitates the discussions in book clubs rather than supporting a specific curricular focus.

Literature Circle Meetings

Once the groups are formed, students read the books. In some classrooms, they meet in their groups and discuss as they read chapter books. They read several chapters and discuss them, reach a consensus on how much they will read for the next meeting, then repeat the process. The discussions help to clarify confusing aspects of the story.

Charlene Klassen found that her fourth-grade students in Fresno, California, needed the encouragement of collaborative meaning building during reading. Many of her Hmong, Laotian, and Cambodian students were still translating from English into their first language as they read. In order to make sense of the story, they needed the support of daily meetings with their group (Short and Klassen 1993).

In other classrooms, students read the entire book before meeting in literature circles. Usually they are given a week or two to read a chapter book, completing the reading during school or for homework. They may meet briefly (about ten minutes) on a daily basis to set goals for their reading and to share their initial responses, questions, and understandings with each other.

Their actual literature circles, however, begin after they have had their own individual "lived through" experiences. This way, they are able to bring broader perspectives to their discussion.

Betsy Brown used both approaches with her fifth-grade students at Huachuca Mountain Elementary School in Sierra Vista, Arizona. She found that groups who read the entire book first participated in more engaging, in-depth discussions than the groups that met while they were reading their book. Discussions that took place as students were reading tended to focus on specific plot details instead of broader issues.

Text set groups focus on a set of books with one copy of each title. These groups usually move continuously between reading and discussing, beginning with students browsing through the books in a set and each choosing one or two books to read alone or with a partner. The group then has an initial meeting. In most cases, the students spend several days reading other books in the set before coming back for further discussion. They often become so interested in the other books in the set that they end up reading all or most of those books.

Remember, the dialogue that characterizes literature circles is the most important part of the meaning-making process.

Inevitably, some students will choose books for literature circles that they cannot yet read by themselves. When this happens, one strategy is to pair those students with more proficient readers from the group. Another possibility is to have the more challenged students read along with a tape of the book. Remember, the dialogue that characterizes literature circles is the most important part of the meaning-making process. I am not overly concerned if students cannot read their discussion books by themselves. I know that as they participate in meaningful literature discussions, they are helped in becoming more thoughtful readers.

Very young readers in kindergarten and first grade offer another challenge. Many are unable to independently read the quality picture books that sustain in-depth discussion, so they need to hear the books read aloud. I have found a number strategies that work. One is to read the book aloud several times throughout a week or so. Students will then come to really know it. If your own time is a concern, making the book available on audiotape is a great solution. "Buddy" readers from older grades or parent volunteers can also read the book aloud. Linda Sheppard (1990) of Phoenix, Arizona, sends the book home in a special packet for three to four days and asks family members to read aloud to her kindergarten students. The packet usually includes a letter to the family, a piece of paper for the child to write or draw a response to the book, and a self-stick note to put on a page the child wants to discuss with group members. Her students bring the book back to school ready to share their thoughts with their literature groups.

I mentioned that young children often need to hear a story several times before they can effectively talk about it in literature circles. Not surprisingly, their discussions are deeper and wider ranging when they work with a story that is familiar to them. In my initial literature circle with first graders, we read the *Three Billy Goats Gruff* by Paul Galdone. We had spent the previous three weeks exploring familiar folktales with "threes" and children had heard these read aloud, acted them out, and spent hours looking through the books on their own. Because of these experiences, our *Billy Goats Gruff* discussion was successful—children talked about the trolls and bullies, who was the bravest billy goat, and how the author made the story more exciting.

Illustration from the *Three Billy Goats Gruff*, ©1973 Paul Galdone. Reprinted by permission of Clarion Books/Houghton Mifflin Company.

Encouraging Conversation

Literature circles begin with friends talking about a book. Children share their favorite parts, retell sections, discuss parts they find confusing, make connections to their own lives or other literature, and engage in social chatter. These first discussions are a time to freely explore a wide range of tentative ideas without focusing on a particular one. Readers need a chance to "muck around" in the literature they read and share their "lived through" experiences before they analyze and critique those experiences. They are not expected to write a summary, answer specific questions, or fill out a story structure worksheet. They simply share their enjoyment and experience with the book.

When I participated in a literature circle of first graders discussing *Rosie's Walk* by Pat Hutchins, they began by sharing favorite pages and laughing over the fox's various predicaments. They talked about what might have happened to the fox at the end of the story and examined the last picture for clues. They debated what kind of homes foxes live in and whether the bees could follow him. They talked about other storybook foxes. They looked at the illustrations and the designs on the animals and talked about why Rosie was different sizes on different pages. The children's excitement influenced the direction of their discussion, which took many twists and turns.

As your students first participate in literature discussions, they may remain silent or make limited comments such as "I liked the story" or "It was boring." They need time, patience, and encouragement along with demonstrations from you and their classmates on ways to think actively and critically about their reading.

Field Notes: Teacher-To-Teacher

To introduce students to literature discussion, I read a picture book aloud and then invite discussion of the story. As students discuss, I take field notes, writing down who made what comment. We then talk as a class about the strategies they used for listening, discussing, and talking with each other. I mention by name what each child said about the story, pointing out the strategies I observed during the discussion. I explain how children added to the discussion by building upon each other's comments, adding details, retelling when we needed clarification, asking questions when we didn't understand, referring back to the text, and so on. I start a list on the board of these discussion strategies and explain we will refer back to these.

Gloria Kauffman
Maldonado Elementary School
Tucson, Arizona

What's on your mind? Don't be surprised if initially your students are reluctant to share their thoughts because they don't believe that you truly care to know what they think. To convince her students otherwise, Carol Hill, a second-grade teacher at the Center for Inquiry in Indianapolis, asked children to choose a book from a stack of picture books that had already been read aloud to the class. She placed an easel next to her chair and as she read a book aloud for a second time, she stopped periodically to ask children, "What's on your mind?" She jotted their comments on the chart. At the end of the book, children chose several comments to discuss further. This strategy has more than one benefit. Children come to understand that books can be read more than once, and they also learn that their teachers do value their opinions (Short and Harste 1996).

Another way to encourage children to share what's on their minds is to place a large piece of brainstorming paper on the table. As students read, they jot or sketch words, images, and connections about their reading on the graffiti board (also called a "sounding off" board). They each take their own section of the paper, although their jottings are not organized in any way. Through this process, they capture their thoughts and images as they read and are able to refer to them later. Look at the graffiti board from Gloria Kauffman's classroom on the next page.

Save the Last Word for Me. Here is (Short and Harste 1996) is yet another strategy that encourages children to share their thoughts. While they are reading, children write down quotes—on a slip of paper or an index card—that they find interesting or significant. On the other side of the paper, they write down why they chose that particular quote. Children bring these quotes to the group and each child chooses one to share. After a child reads a quote, the rest of the group talks about why they think that quote is significant. The child who did the sharing must remain silent—until getting in the "last word" about the quote. Younger children can show an illustration from the book instead of reading a quote. Take a look at the following *Save the Last Word For Me* example for *Bridge to Terabithia*.

Reflective Literature Circles. Often a chapter book read-aloud provides a meaningful shared experience for students. Leslie Kahn (1994) of Robins Elementary School in Tucson, builds on this experience with reflective literature circles. After finishing a read-aloud chapter book that her students particularly enjoyed, she asks them to brainstorm a list of connections to the book. Students then sign up for a reflective literature circle on one of the categories from the list.

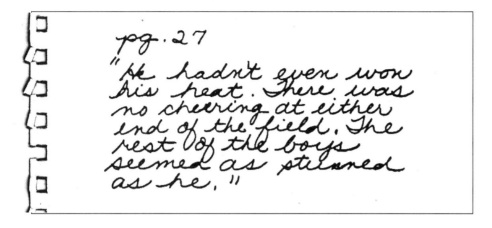

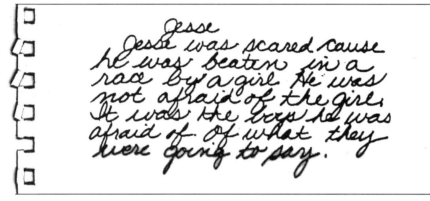

Successful dialogue involves readers in sharing their thinking and in listening to and considering the ideas of other readers.

For example, she read aloud Cynthia Voigt's *Building Blocks* as part of a class focus on family. Afterward, her students brainstormed a list of issues from the book, including fighting in families, time travel, relationships, pollution, and pain. Each group of students chose a particular set of issues to discuss for several days. Their earlier whole class discussions of the book during read-aloud supported the talk in these groups. At the end of the talks, each group presented their insights to the rest of the class.

From Conversation to Dialogue

Once readers have had a chance to share their initial responses in literature circles, the group develops a more specific focus for the discussion and alternates between sharing personal responses and critical dialogue. The focus naturally grows out of the readers' questions and connections and allows them to begin analyzing the book(s) and their responses. Successful dialogue involves readers in sharing their thinking and in listening to and considering the ideas of other readers. Eleven-year-old Tara thoughtfully expressed her impression of successful dialogue in literature circles.

> Some people may read a book and they think a certain thing about a book. I want to know everybody's thoughts and what's going through their mind after they read this book. I've gotten new perspectives talking with others. I get whole new ideas to think about.

In the *Rosie's Walk* literature circle I was involved with, the first graders initial, excited discussion evolved into a debate about whether Rosie knew the fox was behind her. They examined her expression in the illustrations and talked about reasons why she wouldn't want the fox to know she was aware of his presence. They also considered whether or not hens can hear. To this end, they consulted a child from a farm to find out if hens have ears, discussed Rosie's ability to hear, and even told about their own experiences with earaches. Although they didn't reach a final conclusion, they considered a wide range of possibilities, drawing from their experiences and the book's illustrations.

Choice is a key feature of literature circles. Indeed, the direction of the first graders' conversation grew from the group of readers, not from a study guide. Of course teachers can certainly have a say—some read the selected book and make notes on possibilities for discussion. When teachers are members of a literature group, they are participants who contribute to the discussion. Teachers, however, are not always members of the group. In circles without teachers, students are particularly encouraged to develop their own strategies for sustaining discussion and pursuing issues significant to them as children.

Webbing. At the end of the day, I find it helpful to have the groups establish their focus for the following day's discussion. Students are then responsible for preparing for the discussion. Their preparation might involve

- rereading sections of the book
- writing in their literature logs
- further research of their choice.

The goal of these learning events is for the students to clarify what they think about the chosen focus and what they will say in the next group meeting.

In Pamella Sherman's first-grade class at Warren Elementary School in Tucson, students explored different versions of *The Three Bears* for several weeks through read-alouds and drama before they moved into literature circles. I met with five children in a literature circle on the Paul Galdone version of *The Three Bears*. The children shared their favorite pages of the story and explained why they liked them. After twenty-five minutes, the conversation slowed down. I pulled out a large sheet of paper and asked the children to tell me the important ideas about this book that had come up in their sharing. I webbed our brainstorming on the paper—an engagement that is also helpful for times when students are having difficulty finding a focus—and then asked the children which of these ideas they would like to discuss the next day. The first graders in my group chose to discuss whether the little bear was mad or sad because "if he was sad, Goldilocks should have stayed and been his friend."

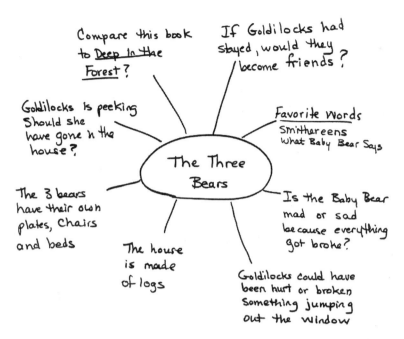

Literature logs. Writing or sketching responses in literature logs gives students a chance to reflect on their individual experiences with books. Gloria Kauffman asks her students to make two to three entries in their logs each week as they read and discuss their books. They are encouraged to write, web, or sketch their responses to what they are reading. Often, students' initial entries are retellings. But gradually, through their experiences in literature groups and through teacher modeling, they learn to include personal connections and evaluations. In some classrooms, students use self-stick notes to mark parts they want to share.

Shiloh   Feb

I think that starving an animal is not how you train a dog. My feeling for the book is sad because treated. like for example the way he gets Kicked around. Why does Judd even hit this dog? Dogs have rights too, I think that Judd lerned from his and it was passed down from Gerertion. I think that dogs are smart too.

Sketch to Stretch. Sometimes particular discussion strategies such as *Sketch to Stretch* (Short and Harste 1996) can support students as they move to dialogue in their discussions. In *Sketch to Stretch*, each child is invited to create a quick sketch of the meaning of the story. Children make sketches of their personal connections and meanings rather than illustrating a scene from the story. Children share their sketches in their literature circles and the other group members talk about the kinds of meanings they see in a particular sketch. The child who drew the sketch then explains his or her depiction.

Comparison charts and story maps. Making comparison charts or story maps are also useful discussion strategies. These work best after students have had a chance to share their initial connections to the book. Comparison charts are effective with text sets or paired books because students can develop categories for comparing the books. They write the categories across the top of the chart and the names of the books along the side. A story map—creating a visual map of the book's story—works well with shared books. The map often develops into a large mural that incorporates all the story elements. Or, the students may show the map as a path that follows the major events of the story.

Some teachers have found it is effective to introduce these discussion strategies at the beginning of the year through read-aloud experiences. As the book is read aloud, they try out a particular strategy as a class and share and compare their efforts. (Chapter books work especially well here.) Other teachers invite their students to try them out with partners using short stories or picture books. As children become familiar with these strategies, they grow more comfortable discussing books. These strategies become options they can choose to use in their literature circles.

Field Notes: Teacher-To-Teacher

Here are some thoughts from our third and sixth grades about presentations in literature circles.

"Presentations helped me to understand the book in different ways. I learned there's not one meaning but many different meanings." –Kristy

"The presentations make all our hard work seem worth it. We weren't just doing a play or something, but we were really sharing a part of ourselves." –Ben

"The meaning of the book isn't complete unless it is shared. We share our knowledge and our feelings." –Luke

"Some teachers think they're the only ones who can teach, but the class can, too. I've learned from presentations that kids can teach." –Geneva

Gloria Kauffman and Kaylene Yoder
Millersburg Elementary School
Millersburg, Indiana

Scheduling Literature Circles

In some classrooms, literature circles are scheduled so that all groups meet at the same time. Teachers move from group to group listening to the discussions. If a group is experiencing difficulty, the teacher may lend her support and join in the conversation. At the end of the literature circle, the groups come together for a class reflection to share the day's discussions. They also talk about any problems that occurred and suggest ways to solve them.

In other classrooms, the literature circle groups meet on a rotating basis. At any one time, some groups meet with the teacher while other students read independently, write in journals, work in centers, or focus on other projects.

Presenting What You've Learned

Group discussions can last anywhere from two days to two weeks. Once a group has finished discussing their book, they decide whether they want to share their book with the class informally or take time to put together a presentation such as a skit or mural (Kauffman and Yoder 1990). Initially, when I worked with children on these presentations, I was discouraged by the "cute" projects they created that were often only peripherally related to their discussion. I found that if I ask children, "What do you want to do?" when they are ready to work on a presentation, they immediately name whatever is popular in the classroom—everyone chooses to act out a skit because that's what's "in" at the moment.

When I worked with a group of fifth graders from Sandy Kaser's classroom who had read *Sarah Bishop* by Scott O'Dell, I asked them, "What do you want other children to learn about your book and discussion? What do you think was most important?" Then, we created a web that summarized their discussions of the book, talked about how they could share these ideas with others, brainstormed a list of many possibilities, and carefully considered which ones would communicate the ideas they wanted to share.

Remember, because the first idea still tended to be whatever was popular in the classroom at the time, it was important not to stop with the first idea but to brainstorm as many as possible.

Literature circles offer all readers the opportunity to become active, critical thinkers.

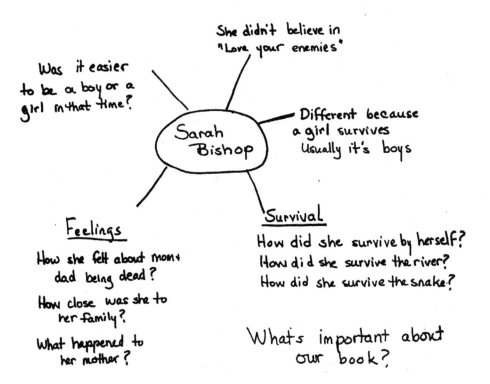

Once they finish a literature circle, children often want time to do further reading—with books related to their group focus, ones that other groups read, or free choice books. They benefit from having several weeks to read broadly before beginning a new literature circle.

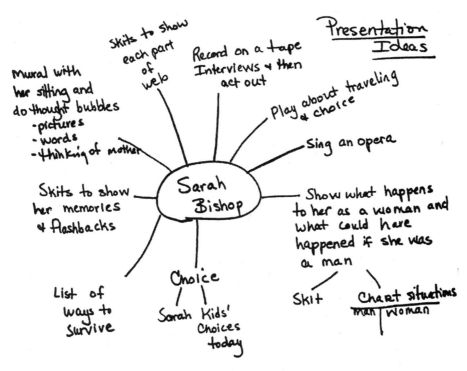

Literature circles offer all readers the opportunity to become active, critical thinkers. The decisions students and teachers make—about the focus of literature circles, types of literature experiences, group membership, selected literature, and organization of the group—influence the kinds of talk and inquiry that evolve from these intensive discussions.

DIALOGUE

How do my students learn through language?

_____

_____

How can I make these engagements even more effective?

_____

_____

What other engagements with learning through language do I want to add to my curriculum?

_____

_____

SHOPTALK

These books are excellent resources for teachers who want to learn more about literature circles. The authors—teachers and teacher educators—share the ways that they integrate literature groups in their classrooms. They discuss the importance of establishing community, organizing the classroom to support "book talk," and making decisions about curriculum and learning.

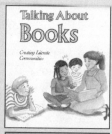

Short, Kathy G. and Kathryn M. Pierce, eds. *Talking About Books: Creating Literate Communities.* Portsmouth, New Hampshire: Heinemann, 1991.

Pierce, Kathryn M. and Carol Gilles, eds. *Cycles of Meaning: Exploring the Potentials of Talk in Learning Communities.* Portsmouth, New Hampshire: Heinemann, 1993.

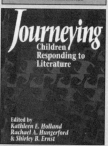

Holland, Kathleen, Rachael Hungerford and Shirley Ernst, eds. *Journeying: Children Responding to Literature.* Portsmouth, New Hampshire: Heinemann, 1993.

Hill, Bonnie C., Nancy Johnson and Katherine S. Noe, eds. *Literature Circles and Response.* Norwood, Massachusetts: Christopher-Gordon, 1995.

Conclusion

While your students engage in dialogue and inquiry through literature, they come to understand and appreciate connections—to others in their classroom community and to the broader worlds of literature and life. In literature circles, not everyone always agrees. Considering other opinions fosters critical reflection, and transforms learning. Your students will become active, critical readers who thoughtfully consider what they read.

Chapter 5

The Authoring Cycle

Since curriculum involves putting our beliefs into action in the classroom, we need a curricular framework that connects our beliefs and practices. We need to choose and organize activities, materials, and practices that are consistent with what we believe about language and learning. When we do this, we bridge our beliefs with our classrooms (Short and Burke 1990).

For many years, my "framework" was the sequential skill and fact charts that were in my teacher's guides and textbooks. I later replaced this linear framework with a grab bag of activities involving reading, writing, and literature. Each day, it felt as if I pulled randomly from this collection. I found myself exhausted and always searching for new theme units, new reading and writing activities, and new experts to provide yet more activities. Eventually, it become clear to me that I needed a framework to support me in thinking, planning, and evaluating curriculum with my students. In Chapters 3 and 4, I shared the framework of learning language, learning about language, and learning through language that helped me think about different literature engagements. In this chapter, I will explore the framework that has become the broader structure I use to think about curriculum and the role of literature in my teaching.

Through my work with Indiana University education professors Carolyn Burke and Jerry Harste, I began to use the authoring cycle as a framework for curriculum (Harste and Short, with Burke 1988; Short and Burke 1990; Short and Harste 1996). I realized that authoring was more than writing—it was a metaphor for the process of creating meaning.

The Authoring Cycle

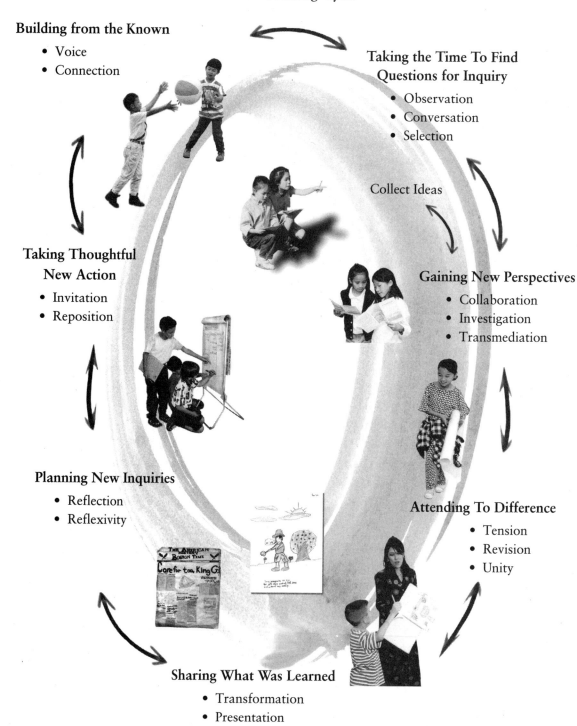

Building from the Known
- Voice
- Connection

Taking the Time To Find Questions for Inquiry
- Observation
- Conversation
- Selection

Collect Ideas

Gaining New Perspectives
- Collaboration
- Investigation
- Transmediation

Taking Thoughtful New Action
- Invitation
- Reposition

Attending To Difference
- Tension
- Revision
- Unity

Planning New Inquiries
- Reflection
- Reflexivity

Sharing What Was Learned
- Transformation
- Presentation

The authoring cycle builds on what children already know—their life experiences. While they build from their own knowledge bases, they need time to explore areas of interest and find the questions that matter to them. As Gloria Kauffman's fifth-grade student Alicia says, "Work at school was hard until I discovered I could change the information and make it have meaning for me. When we do real work, I feel this is real school."

Indeed, in the authoring cycle, students observe the world around them, explore through reading and writing, and talk with other learners. For those of you who are using the Galef Institute's *Different Ways of Knowing* curriculum, you'll recognize this phase of the authoring cycle as Wheel 1, or Exploring What You Already Know.

The authoring cycle builds on what children already know—their life experiences.

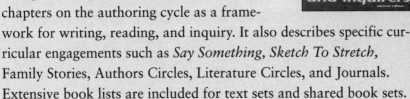

These explorations gradually lead children to questions that they want to explore with others through a focused inquiry. As ten-year-old Marita says, "When I'm finished, I think about what I need to know next." In *Different Ways of Knowing,* this phase corresponds to Wheel 2, Getting Smarter through Research. Students search for answers to their questions using reading, writing, art, music, drama, and other sign systems. Through their investigations and dialogue with others, they encounter new perspectives that nudge them to reconsider—and often revise—their ideas.

Eventually, learners synthesize their understandings and present what they've learned to others. Teachers who are using *Different Ways of Knowing* will identify this phase as Wheel 3, Becoming an Expert, and Wheel 4, Making Connections to Lifelong Learning. When students present what they have learned, they determine what they know and what they still want to explore. Reflecting on what they learned and how they learned it, students plan new inquiries. They also consider new actions they might want to take at home or at school based on their inquiries.

The Authoring Cycle in Action

Let's observe the authoring cycle at work in Junardi Armstrong's second-grade classroom at Cragin Elementary School in Tucson. Cragin is a neighborhood school that serves an ethnically diverse community of working class and middle class families, including many who speak Spanish as their home language. Armstrong is passionate about environmental science, and she continually involves her students in hands-on projects that feature scientific concepts and processes. She used to be less comfortable, however, in her ap-

---

DIALOGUE

What framework currently underlies my curriculum?

_____

_____

What would my classroom look like if I used the authoring cycle or the four learning wheels of *Different Ways of Knowing* as my curricular framework?

_____

_____

---

proaches to reading and writing. We decided to collaborate several years ago, bringing together her strengths in environmental science with my ideas about literature and the authoring cycle (Short and Armstrong 1992).

Within our overarching theme of environments and physical geography, the children zeroed in on life cycles—plant, animal, and human—within particular geographical areas. We began with a broad exploration of cycles in children's lives, such as the cycle children experience every morning as they get ready for school. Then, in small groups, children read books that focused on cycles— the human life cycle in *The Island Boy* by Barbara Cooney, people's impact on each other in *The Quarreling Book* by Charlotte Zolotow, animal life cycles in *The Very Hungry Caterpillar* by Eric Carle, and a food chain in *Jump, Frog, Jump!* by Robert Kalan. Armstrong introduced cycles in nature—producers and consumers, predators and prey, and the water cycle. Based on these experiences, children drew diagrams of the cycles in their lives, literature, and nature.

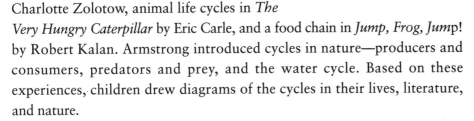

From this broad exploration of cycles, we next thought about ecosystems. What were they? What were their different parts? Where could we see them in action? The children's interests moved our investigations into the rain forest and the Sonoran desert. Beginning with a whole class study of the rain forest and then moving into an authoring cycle around the Sonoran desert, we looked at the relationships between people and other living things in these environments.

Building from the Known: Children's Reading Choices

It is important to remember that the authoring cycle begins with children's own life experiences. They must be able to connect to and build from these experiences if they are to make sense of new ones. In our initial read-alouds, we highlighted books that were similar to the children's own life experiences, such as *Roxaboxen*, Alice McLerran's story about children's imaginary play in the desert. These read-alouds made it easy for them to make personal connections.

We brought many books about the desert into the classroom so the children would have choices, and we watched to see which books they chose during wide reading and recorded their responses during class discussions. What grabbed their attention? What did they understand about the desert? Our goal was to listen to them, learn about their interests and needs, and build on those experiences that were most meaningful to them.

Finding Questions for Inquiry: Reading Engagement

Children explored the desert from many perspectives through lots of wide reading in these initial engagements. They had time to observe, read, and share so they could gradually find topics or questions for further research.

Armstrong's second-grade classroom began to resemble a desert museum and bookstore. Books, displays, and observation centers on the desert occupied every available table and shelf space. Posters, charts, specimens, artifacts, and activities from previous desert units lined the walls of the classroom. We also gathered art prints and music from the media center. Each morning for a week, we gave the children time to explore through reading and observation. Recordings of Navajo flute music and the sounds of desert birds serenaded us. Because the classroom door opened into the courtyard of the school, the children naturally flowed outdoors to study the birds that gathered at the feeding station and to note the plants that grew in the courtyard. After about an hour, we gathered as a class and children shared something they had discovered—a book, an "I wonder" question, or a connection to their lives. Sometimes children shared as partners or small groups before the whole class came together.

Before the children's desert exploration time, we met daily as a class. We opened the meeting with a desert book read-aloud that we thought would connect to children's experiences. When we read Marjorie Weinman Sharmat's *Gila Monsters Meet You at the Airport*, the children loved hearing about a New York City boy's misperceptions of Western life. Following these read-alouds, children were encouraged to share their connections to the book. We also gave short talks on several books from the desert theme set. Just before our meeting ended, the children identified the area they wanted to investigate that morning—and then off they went to explore.

The afternoons carried us into an author study of Byrd Baylor. Art, music, dance, and drama helped us understand and celebrate her books. *When Clay Sings*, with its striking illustrations of American Indian pottery and symbols, inspired children to examine how American Indians use symbols to convey their life in the desert. They thought about their own desert experiences, and using paint and crayons to create abstract shapes and designs, captured their aesthetic feelings about the desert.

After a week of listening to the children and watching them during their explorations, we could tell they were ready to move into a more focused investigation. A read-aloud of *The Desert Is Theirs* by Byrd Baylor, accompanied by Navajo flute music, launched our inquiry. We asked our students to sketch or write ideas on a piece of paper describing their feelings for the desert. We also asked them to identify what they knew about the desert. One child, Thomas, explained his elaborate drawing of birds, scorpions, and ants that live in the desert. He also talked about the feeling of "heatness"—when the sun's rays spread out, blocked only by the mountains.

After students shared their sketches and writing, the class created a web, mapping what they knew and felt about the desert. The web became a springboard for discussions, helping the children clarify what they wanted to study for their focused inquiry.

Gaining New Perspectives: Literature Circles

Previously when Junardi Armstrong and I planned units, we listed books and activities that we thought were important in "covering" the chosen theme. But this time, we began with the students' questions and thought about potential small- and whole-class learning events that would facilitate their inquiries. In that spirit, Byrd Baylor's striking poetry book, *Desert Voices*, was our inspiration to begin a whole class study of children's questions about desert animals. Coyotes, lizards, long-eared jackrabbits, and the industrious cactus wren beckoned to us from the pages. After choosing one animal from Baylor's book, each child researched and worked in a small group with other students who had chosen the same animal. We gave each group copies of their animal poem to read and discuss. The cactus wren group talked about feeling scared when desert creatures were hunting for shade and feeling safe when the wren put her nest in the stickers. They could imagine the feeling of being high in the sky and singing out as the wren flew toward the sun.

The children also prepared choral readings of their poems. Presenting their readings to the class, they used their voices to convey the feelings of fear, warmth, loneliness, power, and hunger that they had discovered through their discussions. Next, we worked as a class to create large webs about our knowledge of each animal.

The children particularly enjoyed the mischievous coyote, so we read aloud several books about coyotes along with a short story from Joe Hayes's *Coyote and*, a collection of Native American traditional literature with stories about the coyote and other desert animals.

Drawing upon these readings and their own experiences, students discussed the character traits of coyotes in the desert and in literature. In literature circles, the children explored Hayes's short story "Coyote and the Rabbit." Gilbert, Ana, Lita, and Joe thought the coyote was stupid to try to trick such a smart rabbit. They webbed the characteristics of the rabbit and the coyote, as well as lessons they thought the coyote learned, such as "Don't trick people" and "Don't stick your nose in other people's business." After they shared their webs, everyone brainstormed further additions to the class coyote web.

Because of the children's enthusiasm about desert animals, Armstrong contacted the local desert museum to find out what kinds of small animals a docent could bring to the classroom. She shared this list with children and they divided into small groups according to animals that most interested them, such as the kangaroo rat, desert tortoise, tarantula, and lizards. The children spent a week in these groups. During the first three days, they researched the animals using posters, reference books, literature, and interviews with children who knew something about that animal. The museum docent brought the animals to the classroom, and children spent time observing their particular animal and asking questions about it. The following day, they charted what they had learned.

As our desert animal study continued, Armstrong and I were pleasantly surprised when it sparked the children's interest in geography. Specifically, they wondered how the physical geography of Arizona compared to that of other geographical areas. Thomas was born on Long Island and could talk about the grasslands and waterways of his birthplace, but most of the children had lived in the Sonoran desert all their lives. To help them understand geographical variations, Armstrong and I put together paired books—books that share a common theme, but are set in different geographical locations. For example, we chose a set that celebrated friendship between people and animals. *Amigo* by Byrd Baylor told the story of a boy and a prairie dog frolicking in the desert, while Brinton Turkle's *Thy Friend, Obadiah* introduced us to a friendship between a boy and a seagull who live on the New England coast. We also paired Barbara Bash's *Desert Giant*, about a day in the life of a saguaro cactus, with *Park Bench*, Fumiko Takeshita's recounting of the day's events as seen through the "eyes" of a Japanese park bench. Although we asked the second graders to discuss connections across these books, they were having difficulty talking in small groups and often spent most of their time "tattling." To address this issue, we used the strategy of reading aloud paired books and discussing them as a class right before the literature circles met. Our demonstrations helped children understand what a meaningful group discussion sounded like, so they were better equipped to participate in their own literature circles.

After these initial whole group discussions, the children chose partners and selected a desert paired book set to read and discuss. Eventually, they met with the two children who had the other book in their set and together, the four children discussed the similarities and differences across the two books. Jorge pointed out that in *Amigo* and *Thy Friend, Obadiah*, "both animals went after the boys to be their friends, but both boys had to train the animals how to act with humans. I wonder if the animals had to train the boys, too." Chela laughed and added, "Both kids were lonely and needed a friend, but the animals wanted to be free."

But keeping in mind that our current focus was geography, the children also examined the paired books for geographical information about the desert and other areas. To help the children explore their questions about the Anasazi and Hohokam, we set up experience centers with pots, clay, and cultural artifacts from these cultures, along with pertinent brochures and books. Finally, as a unifying culmination to our whole class desert study, we spent an exciting day at an outdoor environmental center. We went on a desert hike, found and classified the bones in owl pellets, measured the temperatures of lizards, used pump drills to make holes in clay pendants, and while sitting in a Hohokam pithouse, listened to Byrd Baylor's *One Small Blue Bead*.

Throughout these experiences, students had to put their own ideas into words and images. They also listened to the ideas and perspectives of other learners that, in turn, helped them develop more complex understandings and questions.

Attending to Difference: Revision and Reflection

It is helpful to remember that when students meet in literature circles and inquiry groups, they often explore new perspectives that push them to revise their thinking. Not surprisingly, Armstrong and I found that children needed quiet reflection time—away from the group—to sort out and make sense of the different opinions. During the desert unit, we gave them time at the end of each day to write or sketch what they were learning.

Sharing What Was Learned: Literature Presentations

At various points, children want to present their understandings to others. In "going public," they have to draw upon observations, discussions, and reading, and find a way to convey their understandings to others.

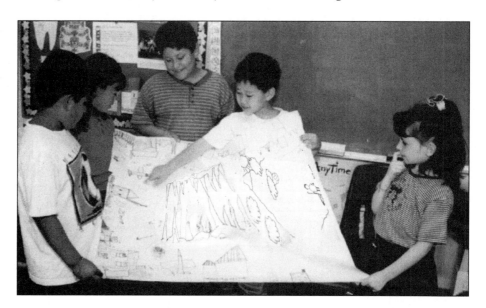

To introduce the process of preparing and giving presentations, Armstrong and I chose a set of paired books involving grandmothers that we had already read aloud and discussed with the children. After listing the comparisons we had made in our earlier class discussion, we brainstormed ways to showcase these comparisons. The children followed this process in their small groups with the desert books. The presentation methods they chose varied—one group developed a comparison chart, another a large mural, and others created diagrams and webs. The final presentations consolidated and celebrated the children's learning, and sparked new questions to explore.

Planning New Inquiries: Reflecting on Reading

Once students have presented their understandings, they gain new perspectives and can reflect more broadly on their learning. At the end of the desert

Field Notes: Teacher-To-Teacher

I used to view presentations as simple sharing sessions in which the kids tell their classmates what they've learned. Recently, however, I have come to place a greater value on them. I believe that presenting allows the kids to use many sign systems—math, music, art, drama, and language. Having more options broadens their thinking about the ideas they are examining. Presenting is not just an end, but also a means to making continued connections with the book and with the children who are observing the presentation. The presentation is not an explanation of an idea or book, but an exploration that is shared by the presenter and built on through the responses of the observers.

Leslie Kahn
Robins Elementary School
Tucson, Arizona

Once students have presented their understandings, they gain new perspectives and can reflect more broadly on their learning.

focus, we spent time reflecting on what the children had learned and how their learning helped them understand their lives, in addition to overall environmental and geographical issues. They especially focused on ways to protect and preserve the desert environment in their neighborhoods. To encourage this reflection, we invited the children to create a portfolio. They put drawings, journal entries, diagrams, webs, and other artifacts into their portfolios, along with a tag explaining why each was important to their learning.

We also talked about what children had learned about their own learning processes, particularly in relation to strategies for research and reading. Children considered what they knew about notetaking, webbing, diagramming, and charting from their experiences studying the desert. We then talked about how they might use these strategies in future learning engagements.

In addition, we discussed strategies for thinking and talking about literature, since this was where children were having the most difficulty. You will remember that we introduced most of these thinking strategies during class read-alouds. To support the development of these strategies, Armstrong helped children who needed it with guided reading, reading in unison with small groups of children, usually less than five. We also included highly predictable books in the classroom library and desert theme set.

Taking Thoughtful New Action

When students reflect on their learning and think about what they understand, they focus on what they know and on what they want to know. In our case, children had many new questions about the desert and other geographical areas that lead to further research. We never "finished" our investigation of cycles, ecosystems, geographical areas, and the desert. We simply pulled together what we knew and determined what still interested us about these topics.

Evaluation within the Authoring Cycle

In the authoring cycle, evaluation is part of the curriculum. It is a reflective stance that teachers and students assume in order to push their learning.

The reflections and invitations to learning that keep the authoring cycle in motion evolve naturally from evaluation. Student and teacher evaluation play key roles in keeping the cycle in a continuous spiral that encompasses ever greater complexities, as our students use literature as a way of knowing about the world.

How do I use evaluation in my classroom?

At the heart of evaluation is the word *value*. Whenever we evaluate, we make a value judgment. We decide what we value for ourselves and others, and make decisions accordingly. Evaluation supports you and your students in working together to gather the information needed to continue learning and inquiring.

This view alters the conventional role of evaluation in the classroom. Traditionally, teachers teach, students respond, and then are tested to see if they learned what was taught. In the authoring cycle, students engage in learning, and with their teachers, evaluate the learning that is occurring. Based on that evaluation, teaching occurs through strategy lessons, invitations to learning, and specific learning events. Evaluation, then, is critical to creating curriculum on an ongoing basis.

Evaluation involves developing a systematic way of gathering, recording, and analyzing what occurs in the classroom. To provide a more specific example of what evaluation might look like within the authoring cycle, let's revisit

Evaluation supports you and your students in working together to gather the information needed to continue learning and inquiring.

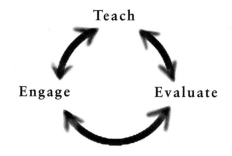

Teach

Engage   Evaluate

Gloria Kauffman, who uses the authoring cycle as her curricular framework. Over time, she has developed many effective evaluation strategies.

Teacher evaluation strategies. Kauffman relies heavily on notes, or anecdotal records, to collect data on her students' responses to literature. She keeps a clipboard or notebook with her at all times and quickly jots down what's going on in the classroom. These notes have especially helped her to understand what is happening in literature circles. She writes down the key ideas that are being discussed and examines her notes so she can evaluate her students' talk. Often, she jots down evaluative comments about the kinds of talk she hears from her students. Here is an example of a literature circle of *Amelia's Road*.

At the end of a particular set of literature circles, Kauffman examines children's literature logs, their discussion webs, and the projects they create for their presentations. She sits down with these materials, along with her own notes, and fills out a *literary comprehension checklist* on each child. These

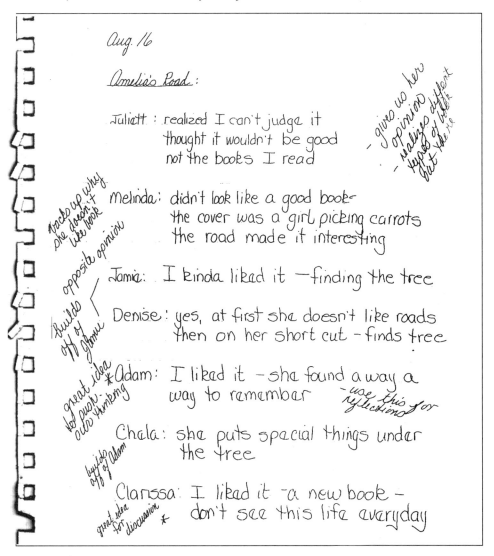

checklists are kept in separate folders or in a large notebook that has a section for each child.

Initially, Kauffman tried to use published checklists, but she eventually abandoned them because the categories weren't appropriate for her students. Instead, she developed her own checklist that evolves as the children in her classroom change in their responses to and understandings of literature.

Comprehension Evaluation Sheet

Literature Discussion and Log Entries	Disc.	Log	Disc.	Log	Disc.	Log
comments on reading material						
retells the main events or summarizes						
webs or lists issues to discuss						
makes predictions						
comments on characters						
discusses illustrations						
states own feelings/opinions						
supports opinions with passages from story						
relates story to own life						
asks questions about things not understood						
I wonder....statements						
sketch to stretch						
charting or graphics						
discusses author's message						
discusses author's style of writing						
builds on comments						
changes own ideas/discovers new ideas						

Presentations

range of possibilities considered			
themes being communicated			
effectiveness of presentations			

Field Notes: Teacher-To-Teacher

Evaluation of a literature program is highly personal. Sometimes students find some literature so personal they choose not to share responses at all. Others choose to share responses that are personal rather than informed by the text, because that's what is called for at that moment. We must never judge a student's response out of the context in which it's made. The most important thing to remember is that students' growth and development are revealed in many ways, in many situations, and we must be ever ready and ever mindful when it appears, so that we can celebrate its occurrence.

Karen Smith
Herrera Elementary School
Phoenix, Arizona

As she examines this checklist, she is particularly interested in whether children are growing and changing. She realizes that children start at different points. For some children, just saying something in the literature circle represents a breakthrough. Other children have learned to move beyond simple retellings to personal connections and evaluative comments.

As students participate in wide reading, Kauffman jots down comments about different students' reading strategies. Sometimes these are written as notes and stored in the child's evaluation folder. Other times she uses a simple checklist, such as the one that follows, to see if she needs to organize a strategy lesson for a particular group. She also notes the kinds of oral reading children are choosing.

At the beginning of the year, Kauffman spends time collecting information on students' interests and attitudes about reading. To find out what her students like to read and what they know about the reading process, she often conducts interviews with small groups of three to four students during the first month of school. She uses questions from the Burke Reading Interview (Goodman, Watson and Burke 1996), such as:

- What do you do when you are reading and come to something you don't know?
- How did you learn to read?
- What would you do to help someone who was having trouble with reading?
- What would you like to do better as a reader?

ORAL READING	PARTNER READING	READERS' THEATRE	PUBLISHED BOOK	READ TO TEACHER CHILD'S CHOICE	READ TO TEACHER LITERATURE CIRCLE BK			ask teacher	picture clues	uses context clues	skips / rereads	skips word	Sounding out / longs,
KATIE													
JASON B.													
JENNIFER													
MICHAEL													
ORPHA													
LUKE													
MARDELL													
SHARILYN													
CHRIS													
CARL													
DARCY													
BRIAN													
FLOYD													
MIRANDA													
JASON P.													
CANDICE													
BEN													
BARBARA													
LORA													

During wide reading, Kauffman notes who is involved in reading and who isn't. Additionally, she's interested in the kinds of books children are choosing. During class discussions of read-aloud books, she takes notes to help her determine her students' current understandings and the ways that they talk about literature. She also asks parents to write a letter about their child and what they have observed in their child's reading and learning strategies. These evaluation strategies help her understand her students. She learns about their strengths as well as areas where she can challenge them.

Self-evaluation strategies. Kauffman recognizes the importance of student self-evaluation. She knows that it helps her students better understand themselves as learners so they can become independent thinkers who monitor their learning. Self-evaluation also provides Kauffman with insights into children's thinking. While reading their comments, she discovers what they value as learners. With this insight, she can make teaching decisions that respond more directly to her students' needs and interests.

Field Notes: Teacher-To-Teacher

I use simple checklists created with the names of the whole class down one side and the top boxes left blank. I then decide what to name my checklist and am able to quickly record my observations. I make many copies of these so I am ready to start kidwatching the moment the children walk into my room at the beginning of the year. I look for children who are shy, assertive, helpers, strugglers. I use these notes to pair students, encouraging those who understand to help those who are lost. I also take field notes about what children are saying and doing continuously throughout the day. These notes help me hear and understand the voices of children. I share these notes with the class to review discussions and ideas. At the end of each week, I remove the checklists from my clipboard and store them in a three-ringed notebook.

Gloria Kauffman
Maldonado Elementary School
Tucson, Arizona

Each morning when the children arrive at school, they write in reflective journals about their previous day. They are invited to write about experiences at school and at home. With this schedule, Kauffman believes her students write more reflectively than they would at the end of the day when they are tired and too close to what they just experienced in school. For example, fifth-grade Rudy wrote an honest impression of Christopher Columbus in a reflective log entry. When students finish writing, they gather for their morning meeting and are invited to share entries with the class. Sharing is strictly invitational.

Christopher Clumbus

I have so many doubts that I don't Know weather to belive this imformation or not. because we don't Know that Clumbus was true or any of this happened it's like on T.V you don't Know if the product works or not

Kauffman also encourages reflection through short verbal class discussions. Frequently throughout the day, she asks a student to turn out the lights and the entire class "freezes." Then, they either reflect from where they are, or quickly gather in the meeting area and take five to ten minutes to reflect on what they are learning and the strategies they are using to learn. For example, after students participated in partner reading for the first time, Kauffman asked them to reflect on the different ways they went about partner reading and how reading with someone else supported them as readers.

These reflections occur as often as every thirty minutes during the first several weeks of school. Initially, most students find reflections difficult. With time and practice, however, they become thoughtful, critical thinkers who are able to step back and analyze their own learning.

TITLES	PREDICTABLE BOOKS	PICTURE BOOKS	CHAPTER BOOKS	INFORMATION BOOKS	CLASS AUTHORS	READERS' THEATRE	POETRY
The Berenstain Bears And The Messy Room	X						
Little Engine That Could	X			X			
Curious George Goes To School	X						
Just Going To The Dentist	X			X			
Lion Is Down In The Dumps	X						
Curious George Bakes A Cake	X						
Just Me And My Little Sister	X						
George and Martha the Misunderstanding	X						
Goose Goofs off	X						
Trains					X		
Pinocchio	X						
Me Too Iguana	X						
The Foot Book	X				X		
Leo The Late Bloomer	X				X		
A Very Scary JackO-Lantern	X						
The Bear Detectives	X				X		
Playground Fun	X				X		
The Three Little Pigs	X				X		
Round & Round & Round		X					
Wher Will I Read?	X				X		
Funny Fingers, Funny Toes	X				X		
Ask Mr. Bear	X				X		
The Bear's Picnic	X						
Hana Upstairs & Hana Downstair	X			X			

Melissa

BOOKS I AM READING

Field Notes: Teacher-To-Teacher

Instead of formal self-evaluation techniques such as forms and checklists, I try to make reflection a natural, daily part of the curriculum. I have found that strategies such as brainstorming, webbing, conferencing, authors circles, literature circles, inquiry groups, class discussions, and various types of journals and learning logs encourage students to reflect on their learning. I want to know what students think and what they value about their learning.

Gloria Kauffman
Maldonado Elementary School
Tucson, Arizona

Students are also responsible for keeping records of their own reading. For example, they keep a list of the books they read during wide reading. Their literature logs provide another important form of self-reflection. As they write in the logs, they are encouraged to think deeply about what they are reading. They can return to these logs to see how their thinking changes over time.

Three times a year, Kauffman asks students to create a portfolio showcasing who they are as readers (Kauffman and Short 1993). First, they gather together all of their charts, webs, literature logs, booklists, literature presentations, and any other artifact relating to themselves as readers. Students share their collections with each other and meet as a class to talk about their observations of what they are doing and thinking as readers. During one such discussion, Clarissa commented, "I skip a word, read the sentence or paragraph, and come back to words I don't know." Adam nodded and offered, "I am willing to make mistakes when I read." Beronica shared one of her strategies, "I retell the story to someone to catch what I missed."

Students then go back to their collections, choosing an item that is the most significant in showing who they are as readers. They meet with a partner and share what they have selected and why they have selected it. Using the descriptions from their meetings, each student writes a half-sheet tag for each item. If they do not have an artifact for an important literature engagement, such as a specific discussion in a literature circle, they simply write the tag or create a quick description, sketch, or web of the engagement, and then add a tag to it.

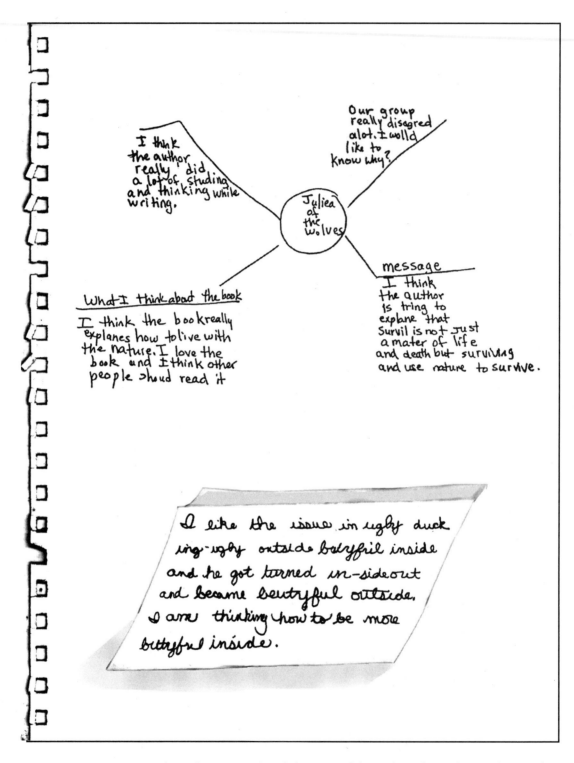

Once students have completed their portfolios, they share them—first with a friend, then with the whole class. The reflection session concludes when each student writes a page outlining their reading goals for the next several months and describing who they are as readers. Mardell, age nine, wrote the portfolio reflection on the following page.

What Kind Of Reader am I?

If a story is written well I am able to guess and predect what will happen next. I then get excited when I read the authors explanation of what happend. I think about probolems that our world faces and I notice how authors solve the problems in thore story book worlds. I am a sereaise reader struggling for answers to solve my personel problem, my sister.

Ugly duckling really had an effect on me. I learned something veary important if you ugly outside and beotyful inside you will probily change and turn beotyful outside and ugly inside My favorite book is The Horse That Came To Brecfest I like horses and I think people should respect them more.

What do I need to read to challenge Myself as a reader?

a) Solve the problem before the story does

b) Read some more nonfiction.

c) Read so that I can read a chapter book without picturs and with the words I can make my own pictures

These portfolios are important reflective tools. Because they are primarily intended to inspire student self-reflection, Kauffman does not evaluate them, she simply reads them to understand more about each child. Although she does give copies of the one-page reflections to the next year's teacher, the portfolio itself belongs to and remains with the child.

Through these various evaluation strategies, Kauffman comes to know her students and the ways in which they read and think about their reading. She is then able to plan learning events to support and challenge her students. In turn, students become aware of their own strategies and understandings and are able to establish goals for their own learning. They participate in decision-making about curriculum and take responsibility for challenging themselves as learners.

DIALOGUE

Do my current evaluation strategies support my curriculum or are they simply for accountability?

_____

_____

What kinds of changes do I want to make in how I evaluate students' engagements with literature?

_____

_____

Conclusion

Learning and teaching are processes of action, reflection, and inquiry. Teachers need time to think and talk with each other, as do students. Too often, new programs are imposed before teachers are given time to think through these ideas for themselves. Accordingly, schools need to provide opportunities for teachers to meet on a regular basis to critically examine their practices and beliefs, and to dialogue with each other (Short et al. 1992).

When we see ourselves as inquirers who pose our own questions and explore possible answers to those questions, we can create lasting changes in our schools. Let's take charge of our learning and make our schools true learning communities. As eleven-year-old Jennifer from Gloria Kauffman's class puts it,

> I did work out of workbooks. I was hoping for a good education. I could tell I was not getting what I wanted. I was wild all the time. I was getting in trouble. I was worrying too much about my friends. Now I like to move around and work with others. I don't like to be alone because I need others to understand me and my ideas. When I work with others, I learn. I need to learn. I need to get along. I share my ideas even if they are not good. I ask questions. The atmosphere in this class has changed my thinking. Others have started to want to learn. I knew if I would try, I would get somewhere.

Professional Bibliography

Allington, Dick. "Content Coverage and Contextual Reading in Reading Groups," *Journal of Reading Behavior 16,* 1984.

Anderson, Richard, Linda Fielding and Paul Wilson. "Growth in Reading and How Children Spend Their Time outside of School," *Reading Research Quarterly 23,* 1988.

Barnes, Douglas. *From Communication to Curriculum.* Portsmouth, New Hampshire: Heinemann, 1976; 1992.

Benedict, Susan and Lenore Carlisle, eds. *Beyond Words: Picture Books for Older Readers and Writers.* Portsmouth, New Hampshire: Heinemann, 1992.

Bridges, Lois. *Assessment: Continuous Learning.* Strategies for Teaching and Learning Professional Library, The Galef Institute. York, Maine: Stenhouse Publishers, 1995.

———. *Creating Your Classroom Community.* Strategies for Teaching and Learning Professional Library, The Galef Institute. York, Maine: Stenhouse Publishers, 1995.

Cadenhead, Kenneth. "Reading Level: A Metaphor that Shapes Practice," *Phi Delta Kappan,* 1987.

Calkins, Lucy McCormick. *Living Between the Lines.* Portsmouth, New Hampshire: Heinemann, 1990.

Commire, Anne. Something about the Author series. Detroit: Gale, 1971–.

Cramer, Eugene and Marietta Castle, eds. *Fostering the Love of Reading: The Affective Domain in Reading Education.* Newark, Delaware: International Reading Association, 1994.

Crawford, Kathleen, Margaret Ferguson, Gloria Kauffman, Julie Laird, Jean Schroeder and Kathy G. Short. "Exploring Historical and Multicultural Perspectives through Inquiry," *If This Is Social Studies, Why Isn't It Boring?*, edited by Stephanie Steffey and Wendy Hood. York, Maine: Stenhouse Publishers, 1994.

Crowell, Caryl. "Living Through War Vicariously with Literature," *Teachers are Researchers: Reflection and Action,* edited by Leslie Patterson, Carol Santa, Kathy Short and Karen Smith. Newark, Delaware: International Reading Association, 1993.

Dewey, John. *Experience and Education.* New York: Collier, 1938.

Freeman, Evelyn and Diane Person, eds. *Using Nonfiction Trade Books in the Elementary Classroom: From Ants to Zeppelins.* Urbana, Illinois: National Council of Teachers of English, 1992.

Freeman. Judy. *Books Kids Will Sit Still for: The Complete Read-Aloud Guide,* 2d ed. New York: R.R. Bowker, 1992.

Freire, Paulo. *Literacy: Reading the Word and the World.* South Hadley, Massachusetts: Bergin and Garvey, 1987.

———. *The Politics of Education.* South Hadley, Massachusetts: Bergin and Garvey, 1985.

Goodman, Kenneth, Patrick Shannon, Yvonne Freeman and Sharon Murphy. *Report Card on Basal Readers.* Katonah, New York: Richard Owen, 1988.

Goodman, Yetta. "Exploring the Power of Written Language through Literature for Children and Adolescents," *The New Advocate 1,* 1988.

Goodman, Yetta, Dorothy Watson and Carolyn Burke. *Reading Strategies: Focus on Comprehension,* 2d ed. Katoneh, New York: Richard Owen, 1996.

Halliday, Michael. *Learning How To Mean.* London: Elsevier, 1975.

———. "Three Aspects of Children's Language Development: Learning Language, Learning through Language, Learning about Language." Paper presented at The Ohio State University, 1984.

Hanssen, Evelyn. "Planning for Literature Circles: Variations in Focus and Structure," *Talking about Books: Creating Literate Communities,* edited by Kathy G. Short and Kathryn Mitchell Pierce. Portsmouth, New Hampshire: Heinemann, 1990.

Harste, Jerome and Kathy Short with Carolyn Burke. *Creating Classrooms for Authors.* Portsmouth, New Hampshire: Heinemann, 1988.

Harwayne, Shelley. *Lasting Impressions: Weaving Literature into the Writing Workshop*. Portsmouth, New Hampshire: Heinemann, 1993.

Heller, Paul G. *Drama as a Way of Knowing*. Strategies for Teaching and Learning Professional Library, The Galef Institute. York, Maine: Stenhouse Publishers, 1995.

Hill, Bonnie C., Nancy Johnson and Katherine S. Noe, eds. *Literature Circles and Response*. Norwood, Massachusetts: Christopher-Gordon, 1995.

Holdaway, Don. *The Foundations of Literacy.* Portsmouth, New Hampshire: Heinemann, 1979.

Holland, Kathleen, Rachael Hungerford and Shirley Ernst, eds. *Journeying: Children Responding to Literature*. Portsmouth, New Hampshire: Heinemann, 1993.

Huck, Charlotte. "The Power of Children's Literature in the Classroom," *Talking about Books: Creating Literate Communities,* edited by Kathy G. Short and Kathryn Mitchell Pierce. Portsmouth, New Hampshire: Heinemann, 1990.

Huck, Charlotte, Susan Hepler and Janet Hickman. *Children's Literature in the Elementary School,* 5th ed. New York: Holt, Rinehart and Winston, 1992.

———. "I Give You the End of a Golden String," *Theory into Practice 22,* 1982.

International Reading Association and National Council of Teachers of English. *Standards for the English Language Arts*. Newark, Delaware: International Reading Association and Urbana, Illinois: National Council of Teachers of English, 1996.

Kahn, Leslie. "Mathematics as Life: Children's Response to Literature," Unpublished thesis, University of Arizona, 1994.

Kahn, Leslie, Paul Fisher and Dana Pitt. "Teacher, Artist, Lawyer, Kids: Cycles of Collaboration and the Holocaust," *If This Is Social Studies, Why Isn't It Boring?,* edited by Stephanie Steffey and Wendy Hood. York, Maine: Stenhouse, 1994.

Kaser, Sandy. "Creating a Learning Environment that Invites Connections," *If This Is Social Studies, Why Isn't It Boring?,* edited by Stephanie Steffey and Wendy Hood. York, Maine: Stenhouse, 1994.

———. "Exploring Cultural Identity: Creating a Learning Environment that Invites Cultural Connections through Family Studies, Inquiry, and Children's Literature." Unpublished thesis, University of Arizona, 1994.

Kauffman, Gloria. "Creating a Collaborative Environment," *Creating Classrooms for Authors and Inquirers*, edited by Kathy G. Short and Jerome Harste. Portsmouth, New Hampshire: Heinemann, 1996.

Kauffman, Gloria and Kathy Short. "Self-Evaluation Portfolios: A Device To Empower Learners," *Windows into Literacy: Assessing Learners, K-8,* edited by Lynn Rhodes and Nancy Shanklin. Portsmouth, New Hampshire: Heinemann, 1993.

Kauffman, Gloria and Kaylene Yoder. "Celebrating Authorship: A Process of Collaborating and Creating Meaning," *Talking about Books: Creating Literate Communities,* edited by Kathy G. Short and Kathryn Mitchell Pierce. Portsmouth, New Hampshire: Heinemann, 1990.

Lipson, Eden. *The New York Times Parents' Guide to the Best Books for Children.* New York: Times Books, 1991.

Lloyd, Pamela. *How Writers Write.* Portsmouth, New Hampshire: Heinemann, 1987.

Moll, Luis. "Bilingual Classroom Studies and Community Analyses: Some Recent Trends," *Educational Researcher 21,* 1992.

Morrow, Leslie. "Promoting Voluntary Reading," *Handbook of Research on Teaching the English Language Arts,* edited by James Flood, Julie Jensen, Diane Lapp and James Squire, pp. 681-689. New York: Macmillan, 1991.

National Institute of Education. *Becoming a Nation of Readers: The Report of the Commission on Reading.* Washington, DC: National Institute of Education, 1985.

Ohanian, Susan. *Math as a Way of Knowing.* Strategies for Teaching and Learning Professional Library, The Galef Institute. York, Maine: Stenhouse Publishers, 1995.

Page, Nick. *Music as a Way of Knowing.* Strategies for Teaching and Learning Professional Library, The Galef Institute. York, Maine: Stenhouse Publishers, 1995.

Peterson, Ralph and Mary Ann Eeds. *Grand Conversations: Literature Groups in Action.* New York: Scholastic, 1990.

Pierce, Kathryn Mitchell. "Getting Started: Establishing a Reading/Writing Classroom," *Creating Classrooms for Authors and Inquirers,* edited by Kathy G. Short and Jerome Harste. Portsmouth, New Hampshire: Heinemann, 1995.

Pierce, Kathryn Mitchell and Carol Gilles, eds. *Cycles of Meaning: Exploring the Potentials of Talk in Learning Communities.* Portsmouth, New Hampshire: Heinemann, 1993.

Rhodes, Lynn. "I Can Read!: Predictable Books as Resources for Reading and Writing Instruction," *The Reading Teacher 345,* 1981.

Rosenblatt, Louise. *The Reader, the Text, the Poem.* Carbondale, Illinois: Southern Illinois University Press, 1978.

Roser, Nancy and Miriam Martinez, eds. *Book Talk and Beyond: Children and Teachers Respond to Literature.* Newark, Delaware: International Reading Association, 1995.

Saul, Wendy and Sybille Jagusch, eds. *Vital Connections: Children, Science, and Books.* Portsmouth, New Hampshire: Heinemann, 1991.

Shannon, Patrick and Kenneth Goodman. *Basal Readers: A Second Look.* Katonah, New York: Richard Owen, 1994.

Sheppard, Linda. "Literacy Environments that Support Strategic Readers," *Bridges to Literacy,* edited by Diane DeFord, Carol Lyons and Gay Su Pinnell. Portsmouth, New Hampshire: Heinemann, 1991.

————. "Our Class Knows Frog and Toad: An Early Childhood Literature-Based Classroom," *Talking about Books: Creating Literate Communities,* edited by Kathy G. Short and Kathryn Mitchell Pierce. Portsmouth, New Hampshire: Heinemann, 1990.

Short, Kathy G. "Making Connections across Literature and Life," *Journeying: Children Responding to Literature,* edited by Kathleen Holland, Rachael Hungerford and Shirley Ernst. Portsmouth, New Hampshire: Heinemann, 1992.

Short, Kathy G., ed. *Research and Professional Resources in Children's Literature: Piecing a Patchwork Quilt.* Newark, Delaware: International Reading Association, 1995.

Short, Kathy G. and Junardi Armstrong. "More than Facts: Exploring the Role of Talk in Classroom Inquiry," *Cycles of Meaning: Exploring the Potential of Talk in Learning Communities,* edited by Kathryn Mitchell Pierce and Carol Gilles. Portsmouth, New Hampshire: Heinemann, 1993.

————. "Moving Toward Inquiry: Integrating Literature into the Science Curriculum," *The New Advocate 6,* 1993.

Short, Kathy G. and Carolyn Burke. *Creating Curriculum: Teacher and Students as a Community of Learners.* Portsmouth, New Hampshire: Heinemann, 1990.

Short, Kathy, G., Kathleen Crawford, Leslie Kahn, Sandy Kaser, Charlene Klassen and Pamella Sherman. "Teacher Study Groups: Exploring Literacy Issues through Collaborative Dialogue," *Forty-First Yearbook of the National Reading Conference,* edited by Donald Leu and Charles Kinzer. Chicago: National Reading Conference, 1992.

Short, Kathy G. and Jerome Harste. *Creating Classroom for Authors and Inquirers.* Portsmouth, New Hampshire: Heinemann, 1996.

Short, Kathy G. and Charlene Klassen. "Literature Circles: Hearing Children's Voices," *Children's Voices: Talk in the Classroom,* edited by Bernice Cullinan. Newark, Delaware: International Reading Association, 1993.

Short, Kathy, G., Jean Schroeder, Julie Laird, Gloria Kauffman, Margaret Ferguson and Kathleen Crawford. *Learning Together through Inquiry*. York, Maine: Stenhouse, 1996.

Slaughter, Judith Pollard. *Beyond Storybooks: Young Children and the Shared Book Experience*. Newark, Delaware: International Reading Association, 1993.

Smith, Frank. *Joining the Literacy Club*. Portsmouth, New Hampshire: Heinemann, 1988.

———. *Reading without Nonsense*, 3rd ed. New York: Teachers College Press, 1997.

Smith, Karen. "Entertaining a Text: A Reciprocal Process," *Talking about Books: Creating Literate Communities*, edited by Kathy G. Short and Kathryn Pierce. Portsmouth, New Hampshire: Heinemann, 1990.

Sulzby, Elizabeth. "The Development of the Young Child and the Emergence of Literacy," *Handbook of Research on Teaching the English Language Arts*, edited by James Flood, Julie Jensen, Diane Lapp and James Squire. New York: Macmillan, 1991.

Trelease, Jim. *The New Read-Aloud Handbook*. New York: Penguin, 1989.

Tunnell, Michael and Richard Ammon, eds. *The Story of Ourselves: Teaching History through Children's Literature*. Portsmouth, New Hampshire: Heinemann, 1993.

Watson, Dorothy and Suzanne Davis. "Readers and Texts in a Fifth-Grade Classroom," *Literature in the Classroom*, edited by Ben Nelms. Urbana, Illinois: National Council of Teachers of English, 1988.

Children's Bibliography

Picture Books

Ackerman, Karen. *Song and Dance Man*. Illustrated by Stephen Gammell. New York: Scholastic, 1988. Grandpa recreates the magic of vaudeville for his grandchildren in an attic performance. Caldecott Medal.

Ahlberg, Janet and Allen Ahlberg. *The Jolly Postman*. Boston: Little, Brown, 1986. The postman delivers letters to fairytale characters that readers can remove from real envelopes in the book.

Arnold, Tedd. *The Signmaker's Assistant*. New York: Dial, 1992. A young signmaker's apprentice dreams of having his own sign shop but creates havoc when he is left in charge.

Bash, Barbara. *Desert Giant*. Boston: Little, Brown, 1989. This book captures the life cycle of the saguaro cactus and all of the creatures who depend on the cactus for survival.

Baylor, Byrd. *Amigo*. Illustrated by Garth Williams. New York: Macmillan, 1963. Desperately wanting a pet to love, a boy decides to tame a prairie dog who has already decided to tame the boy for his own pet.

———. *The Desert Is Theirs*. Illustrated by Peter Parnall. New York: Macmillan, 1975. A poem stresses the love that the Papago Indians (Tohono O'odham) have for their desert home.

———. *Desert Voices*. Illustrated by Peter Parnall. New York: Scribner, 1981. Ten creatures from the desert offer their viewpoints on their surroundings.

————. *I'm in Charge of Celebrations*. Illustrated by Peter Parnall. New York: Scribner, 1986. A desert dweller uses her diary to keep track of special days to celebrate, like the day she saw a triple rainbow and the time she encountered a coyote.

————. *One Small Blue Bead*. Illustrated by Ron Himler. New York: Scribner, 1992. A boy makes it possible for an old man in his tribe to search for other people in far-off places.

————. *When Clay Sings*. Illustrated by Tom Bahti. New York: Macmillan, 1972. A poetic telling of the ancient way of life, through the designs on prehistoric Indian pottery from the southwestern desert of what is now the United States.

Brisson, Pat. *Your Best Friend, Kate*. New York: Bradbury, 1989. A girl writes letters to her best friend about her experiences during a car trip.

Bunting, Eve. *A Day's Work*. Illustrated by Ron Himler. New York: Clarion, 1994. When Francisco, a young Mexican American boy, tries to help his grandfather find work, he discovers that even though the old man cannot speak English, he has something even more valuable to teach Francisco.

————. *The Wednesday Surprise*. Illustrated by Donald Carrick. New York: Clarion, 1989. A seven-year-old girl teaches her grandmother to read.

Carle, Eric. *The Very Hungry Caterpillar*. New York: Philomel, 1969. A predictable pattern book that presents the life cycle of a caterpillar who eats his way through the pages.

Cherry, Lynne. *The Great Kapok Tree*. New York: Trumpet, 1990. The animals who depend on the rain forest for their existence speak in a dream to the man who has come to cut down their trees.

Cohen, Miriam. *When Will I Read?* Illustrated by Lillian Hoban. New York: Greenwillow, 1977. A young child in a multiethnic classroom is concerned about when he will learn to read.

Cooney, Barbara. *The Island Boy*. New York: Viking, 1989. Here is the life story of a boy growing up during an earlier time on an island in New England.

Cummings, Pat. *Talking with Artists*. New York: Bradbury, 1992. These interviews with fourteen illustrators of children's books include examples of their work as children and as adults.

————. *Talking with Artists, Volume II*. New York: Simon & Schuster, 1995. In this second compilation, we meet thirteen children's book illustrators reflecting on their current work and their childhood memories.

de Paola, Tomie. *Now One Foot, Now the Other*. New York: Trumpet, 1981. A child whose grandfather helped him learn to walk helps Grandpa relearn the skill after he suffers a stroke.

Dorros, Arthur. *Abuela*. Illustrated by Elise Kleven. New York: Trumpet, 1991. A young girl takes an imaginary flight over New York City with her Puerto Rican grandmother.

Emberely, Michael. *Ruby*. Boston: Little, Brown, 1990. A modern variant of Little Red Riding Hood in which Ruby, a small mouse, must outwit a cat on the way to her grandmother's apartment in the city.

French, Fionna. *Snow White in New York*. Oxford: Oxford University, 1986. Fionna presents a modern variant of the traditional Snow White tale set in New York City.

Galdone, Paul. *Rumpelstiltskin*. Boston: Houghton Mifflin, 1985. The traditional tale of a miller's daughter who spins gold with the help of a little man who demands something in return.

———. *The Three Bears*. New York: Clarion, 1985. The traditional tale is told of Goldilocks' surprise visit to the home of the three bears.

———. *The Three Billy Goats Gruff*. New York: Seabury, 1973. Three billy goats must cross the mean troll's bridge to get to green grass in this traditional tale.

Goor, Ron and Nancy Goor. *Signs*. New York: Crowell, 1983. Text and photographs present familiar signs in daily life.

Greenfield, Eloise. *Grandma's Joy*. Illustrated by Carole Byard. New York: Philomel, 1980. A little girl tries to cheer up her despondent grandmother by reminding her of what is most important in her life.

Hazen, Barbara. *Tight Times*. Illustrated by Trina Schart Hyman. New York: Puffin, 1979. A family in the city experiences hard times when the father loses his job.

Heide, Florence P. and Judith H. Gilliland. *The Day of Ahmed's Secret*. Illustrated by Ted Lewin. New York: Scholastic, 1992. The story follows a boy through his day of work in Cairo and his excitement of sharing his secret with his family—he can write his own name.

Heins, Paul. *Snow White*. Illustrated by Trina Schart Hyman. Boston: Little, Brown, 1974. A romantic traditional tale of Snow White and her life among the seven dwarfs.

Hoban, Tana. *I Read Signs*. New York: Greenwillow, 1983. Hoban's book introduces signs and symbols frequently seen along the street.

———. *I Walk and Read*. New York: Greenwillow, 1984. A child goes for a walk and sees many familiar signs along the way.

Hutchins, Pat. *The Tale of Thomas Mead*. New York: Greenwillow, 1980. This is the humorous tale of Thomas Mead, who refuses to learn how to read and ends up in jail because he can't read signs.

————. *Rosie's Walk*. New York: Macmillan, 1968. The humorous misadventures of a fox chasing a hen are told primarily through illustrations.

————. *Titch*. New York: Macmillan, 1971. This predictable pattern book relates the problems of being the youngest child.

————. *Tom and Sam*. New York: Macmillan, 1968. Tom and Sam are two friends who become jealous as each one tries to outdo the other.

Hyman, Trina Schart. *Little Red Riding Hood*. New York: Holiday, 1983. This is a traditional retelling of the Grimm tale of a young girl who goes to visit her grandmother, and the wolf who threatens her.

Innocenti, Roberto. *Rose Blanche*. Mankato, Minnesota: Creative Education, 1985. A young village girl discovers a concentration camp in Germany and tries to help feed the starving children.

Johnson, Angela. *Tell Me a Story, Mama*. Illustrated by David Soman. New York: Orchard, 1989. A small girl and her mother recall the child's favorite stories about Mama's childhood.

Johnson, Dolores. *Papa's Stories*. New York: Macmillan, 1994. Kari loves to have her father read to her, but then she discovers that he cannot read and is making up the stories.

Johnston, Tony. *Amber on the Mountain*. Illustrated by Robert Duncan. New York: Dial, 1994. Isolated on a mountain, Amber meets a girl from the city who gives her the determination to learn to read and write.

Kalan, Robert. *Jump, Frog, Jump!* Illustrated by Byron Barton. New York: Greenwillow, 1981. This is a predictable book that uses a cumulative pattern to tell the story of a frog who escapes from a whole series of dangers.

Lobel, Arnold. *Fables*. New York: Harper, 1980. Lobel's witty book of original fables tells stories of all kinds of animals, from a crocodile to an ostrich. Caldecott Medal.

Martin, Bill, Jr. *Brown Bear, Brown Bear*. Illustrated by Eric Carle. New York: Holt, 1983. Martin's patterned language book of questions and responses is about what various animals see.

Martin, Bill, Jr. and John Archambault. *Knots on a Counting Rope*. Illustrated by Ted Rand. New York: Holt, 1987. Boy-Strength-of-Blue-Horses and his grandfather tell stories about the young boy's birth, his first horse, and an exciting horse race.

McLerran, Alice. *Roxaboxen*. Illustrated by Barbara Cooney. New York: Lothrop, 1991. Children turn the desert into an imaginary playground by creating their own town.

Mochizuki, Ken. *Baseball Saved Us.* Illustrated by Dom Lee. New York: Lee & Low, 1993. A young Japanese American boy deals with the prejudice he faces in an internment camp during World War II through baseball.

Mora, Pat. *A Birthday Basket for Tia.* Illustrated by Cecily Lang. New York: Macmillan, 1992. With the help and interference of her cat Chica, Cecilia prepares a surprise gift for her great-aunt's birthday.

Moser, Barry. *Tucker Pfeffercorn.* Boston: Little, Brown, 1994. Barry Moser presents a modern retelling of the Rumpelstiltskin tale with a Southern setting and a spunky heroine.

Nixon, Joan L. *If You Were a Writer.* Illustrated by Bruce Degen. New York: Four Winds, 1988. Melia tells her writer mother she'd like to be a writer too, and as the day progresses she receives many helpful suggestions.

Oberman, Sheldon. *The Always Prayer Shawl.* Illustrated by Ted Lewin. Honesdale, Pennsylvania: Boyds Mill, 1994. A prayer shawl is handed down from grandfather to grandson in this story of Jewish tradition and the passage of generations.

O'Neill, Catherine. *Mrs. Dunphy's Dog.* New York: Viking, 1987. A dog learns to read and finds out that all stories are not to be believed.

Ormerod, Jan. *Reading.* New York: Lothrop, 1985. This world book depicts a father attempting to read his book while a toddler crawls in and out of his legs and finally rests in his arms, reading too.

Peek, Merle. *Mary Wore Her Red Dress and Henry Wore His Green Sneakers.* New York: Clarion, 1991. Based on the popular song, this book uses predictable patterns with children's names and the clothes they are wearing.

Polacco, Patricia. *Aunt Chip and the Great Triple Creek Dam Affair.* New York: Philomel, 1996. This is a humorous commentary on a town which is so obsessed with television that they have forgotten how to read.

———. *The Bee Tree.* New York: Philomel, 1993. When a young girl is bored with reading, her grandfather suggests they go in search of a bee tree.

Sendak, Maurice. *Where the Wild Things Are.* New York: Harper, 1963. Max goes on a mischievous and imaginary journey to find and conquer the wild things. Caldecott Medal.

Shannon, George. *Lizard's Song.* Illustrated by Jose Aruego and Ariane Dewey. New York: Greenwillow, 1981. A lizard tries unsuccessfully to teach the lizard's song to a bear until he finally realizes that the bear needs his own song.

Sharmat, Marjorie W. *Gila Monsters Meet You at the Airport.* Illustrated by Byron Barton. New York: Viking, 1980. This story presents the misperceptions of a boy from New York City about life in the West.

Steig, William. *Sylvester and the Magic Pebble.* New York: Trumpet, 1969. A magic pebble causes a donkey to turn into a rock and his frantic parents are unable to find him. Caldecott Medal.

Steptoe, John. *The Story of Jumping Mouse.* New York: Mulberry, 1972. This is the Great Plains Indian tale of a mouse who jeopardizes his own dream to help others in need.

Stolz, Mary. *Storm in the Night.* Illustrated by Pat Cummings. New York: Harper & Row, 1988. When a storm cuts off the electricity, a boy and his grandfather share stories about fear of the dark.

Surat, Michelle. *Angel Child, Dragon Child.* Illustrated by Vo-Dinh Mai. New York: Scholastic, 1983. A young Vietnamese girl is teased by her new classmates in America.

Takeshita, Fumiko. *Park Bench.* New York: Kane/Miller, 1989. The white bench in a Japanese park provides pleasure for many people during a sunny day.

Turkle, Brinton. *Thy Friend, Obadiah.* New York: Viking, 1969. Obadiah's new friend is a seagull who embarrasses the boy by following him everywhere in Nantucket in the early nineteenth century.

Wheatley, Nadia and Donna Rawlins. *My Place.* Brooklyn: Kane/Miller, 1989. Each double-page spread revisits the same neighborhood in Australia through many decades to a time before the Europeans came.

Wild, Margaret. *Let the Celebrations Begin.* Illustrated by Julie Vivas. New York: Orchard, 1991. Even as they hope and despair of their liberation day, Polish women in a concentration camp are determined to make toys for the children.

Williams, Vera. *A Chair for My Mother.* New York: Mulberry, 1982. A little girl, her mother, and grandmother have lost their home in a fire and are saving coins in a jar to buy a comfortable armchair.

———. *Cherries and Cherry Pits.* New York: Greenwillow, 1986. A girl uses her magic marker to tell stories about people who like cherries.

Yashima, Taro. *Crow Boy.* New York: Viking, 1955. Chibi is an outcast who is teased by other children until a teacher discovers that he knows every call crows make. Set in Japan.

Zolotow, Charlotte. *The Quarreling Book.* Illustrated by Arnold Lobel. New York: Harper, 1963. It's one of those days when everything seems to go from bad to worse as each member of the family passes on their bad mood to someone else, until the family dog gets everything back on the right track.

Chapter Books

Alexander, Lloyd. *The Black Cauldron*. New York: Holt, 1965. Taran and his companions seek to find and destroy an evil cauldron from the Land of Death in this book from the Prydain series.

Babbit, Natalie. *Tuck Everlasting*. New York: Trumpet, 1975. A girl must decide whether she will drink from a spring that has given eternal life to a family she befriends.

Birdseye, Tom. *Just Call Me Stupid*. New York: Holiday, 1993. Terrified of failing and believing that he is stupid, a fifth grader who has never learned to read begins to believe in himself with the help of a new neighborhood girl and a teacher at school.

Buss, Fran Leeper. *Journey of the Sparrows*. New York: Lodestar, 1991. A family of political refugees from El Salvador must struggle to survive and avoid deportation in Chicago.

Byars, Betsy. *The Pinballs*. New York: Scholastic, 1977. Three foster children who feel their lives are out of control gain security from each other and their foster parents.

Fox, Paula. *Monkey Island*. New York: Orchard, 1991. Clay is homeless and tries to survive on the streets when his mother disappears from their welfare hotel.

George, Jean Craighead. *Julie of the Wolves*. New York: Harper, 1972. Julie is caught between Eskimo and white cultures as she tries to survive on the Arctic tundra with the help of a pack of wolves. Newbery Medal.

———. *My Side of the Mountain*. New York: Dutton, 1959. A New York City boy runs away from his family to prove he can survive completely on his own in a mountain wilderness for a year.

Greene, Bette. *Summer of My German Soldier*. New York: Dial, 1973. A young Jewish girl faces persecution when she befriends a German prisoner of war in a small town in Arkansas.

Hayes, Joe. *Coyote and*. Santa Fe, New Mexico: Mariposa, 1983. Joe Hayes presents a collection of Native American traditional stories about the trickster coyote.

Klein, Robin. *Penny Pollard's Diary*. Melbourne, Australia: Oxford University, 1983. This story of a friendship between an elderly woman and a rebellious young girl is told through the girl's diary.

Konigsburg, E. L. *From the Mixed-Up Files of Mrs. Basil E. Frankweiler*. New York: Atheneum, 1970. To solve a mystery, two children run away from home and live in the Metropolitan Museum of Art. Newbery Medal.

Lowry, Lois. *The Giver.* Boston: Houghton Mifflin, 1993. A young boy is given the gift of memory in a future utopian community that is devoid of conflict and conscience. Newbery Medal.

———. *Number the Stars.* Boston: Houghton Mifflin, 1989. Danish citizens try to save their Jewish friends by smuggling them past the Nazis in 1943. Newbery Medal

Martin, Ann M. The Babysitter's Club series. New York: Scholastic, 1986–.

MacLachlan, Patricia. *Sarah, Plain and Tall.* New York: Harper, 1985. Motherless Caleb and Anna are delighted when Papa's advertisement for a mail-order bride brings Sarah, on a trial basis, to their pioneer home on the prairie. Newbery Medal.

McSwigan, Marie. *Snow Treasure.* New York: Dutton, 1942. A retelling of a true adventure in which children smuggle gold past the Nazis in Norway.

O'Dell, Scott. *Island of the Blue Dolphins.* New York: Dell, 1960. Karana, an Indian girl, is left behind on an island off the coast of California and survives by herself for eighteen years. Newbery Medal.

———. *Sarah Bishop.* Boston: Houghton Mifflin, 1980. Sarah bitterly withdraws from human contact when opposing forces in the Revolutionary War kill her father and her brother.

Paterson, Katherine. *Bridge to Terabithia.* New York: Trumpet, 1977. The story of a friendship between a boy and a girl who create an imaginary world that sustains Jess when Leslie dies. Newbery Medal.

Paulsen, Gary. *Hatchet.* New York: Trumpet, 1987. When the pilot suffers a fatal heart attack, Brian must survive alone in the Canadian wilderness.

Pitts, Paul. *Racing the Sun.* New York: Avon, 1988. Brandon has grown up in the city and sees himself as just a regular kid until his grandfather's health forces him to leave the Navajo reservation and move into Brandon's room.

Reiss, Johanna. *The Upstairs Room.* New York: Crowell, 1972. This is a true story of a Jewish girl's experiences hiding from the Nazis.

Serraillier, Ian. *Escape from Warsaw.* New York: Scholastic, 1990. Set in Poland during World War II, three Jewish boys go in search of their families.

Spinelli, Jerry. *Maniac Magee.* New York: Scholastic, 1990. A homeless boy becomes a legend as he brings together a racially divided town and searches for a home. Newbery Medal.

Stine, R. L. Goosebumps series. New York: Scholastic, 1992–.

Taylor, Mildred. *Roll of Thunder, Hear My Cry.* New York: Dial, 1976. Set in Mississippi during the Depression, a black family encounters discrimination and prejudice, but is strong in their love for each other and the land they own. Newbery Medal.

Temple, Frances. *Grab Hands and Run.* New York: Orchard, 1993. The journey to Canada of an El Salvadoran family who must flee government soldiers after the father disappears.

Uchida, Yoshika. *A Jar of Dreams.* New York: Atheneum, 1981. Set during the Depression, Rinko has to deal with prejudice toward her Japanese American family and her own embarrassment of her heritage.

Voigt, Cynthia. *Building Blocks.* New York: Fawcett, 1984. Brann is upset with his parent's constant fighting, but comes to understand his father when he travels back in time and meets his father as a child.

Yolen, Jane. *The Devil's Arithmetic.* New York: Trumpet, 1988. A time travel historical novel that begins in the present when Hannah opens the door at the family's celebration of Passover and suddenly finds herself in a Polish village in the 1940s.

Poetry

de Regniers, Beatrice. *Sing a Song of Popcorn.* New York: Scholastic, 1988. An anthology of poems on many different topics, this book is illustrated by nine Caldecott Medal artists.

Hopkins, Lee Bennett, ed. *Good Books, Good Times.* New York: Harper, 1990. This is a picture book collection of poems about books and reading.

Little, Jean. *Hey World, Here I Am!* New York: Harper & Row, 1986. Poetry and short stories celebrate reading and writing in the life of a twelve-year-old girl.

Livingston, Myra C. *Poems for Grandmothers.* New York: Holiday, 1990. This is a collection of eighteen poems about grandmothers, great-grandmothers and step-grandmothers of various races, ages, and economic backgrounds.

Kennedy, X. J. *Knock at a Star: A Child's Introduction to Poetry.* Boston: Little, Brown, 1982. This anthology of poems is organized to help children understand poetry.

Prelutsky, Jack, ed. *The Random House Book of Poetry for Children.* Illustrated by Arnold Lobel. New York: Random, 1983. This anthology contains over five hundred poems, divided according to theme.

Professional Associations and Publications

The American Alliance for Health, Physical Education, Recreation, and Dance (AAHPERD)
Journal of Physical Education, Recreation, and Dance
1900 Association Drive
Reston, Virginia 22091

American Alliance for Theater and Education (AATE)
AATE Newsletter
c/o Arizona State University Theater Department
Box 873411
Tempe, Arizona 85287

American Association for the Advancement of Science (AAAS)
Science Magazine
1333 H Street NW
Washington, DC 20005

American Association of Colleges for Teacher Education (AACTE)
AACTE Briefs
1 DuPont Circle NW, Suite 610
Washington, DC 20036

American Association of School Administrators (AASA)
The School Administrator
1801 North Moore Street
Arlington, Virginia 22209

Association for Childhood Education International (ACEI)
Childhood Education: Infancy Through Early Adolescence
11141 Georgia Avenue, Suite 200
Wheaton, Maryland 20902

Association for Supervision and Curriculum Development (ASCD)
Educational Leadership
1250 North Pitt Street
Alexandria, Virginia 22314

The Council for Exceptional Children (CEC)
Teaching Exceptional Children
1920 Association Drive
Reston, Virginia 22091

Education Theater Association (ETA)
Dramatics
3368 Central Parkway
Cincinnati, Ohio 45225

International Reading Association
(IRA)
The Reading Teacher
800 Barksdale Road
Newark, Delaware 19714

Music Educators National Conference
(MENC)
Music Educators Journal
1806 Robert Fulton Drive
Reston, Virginia 22091

National Art Education Association
(NAEA)
Art Education
1916 Association Drive
Reston, Virginia 22091

National Association for the Education
of Young Children (NAEYC)
Young Children
1509 16th Street NW
Washington, DC 20036

National Association of Elementary
School Principals (NAESP)
Communicator
1615 Duke Street
Alexandria, Virginia 22314

National Center for Restructuring
Education, Schools, and Teaching
(NCREST)
Resources for Restructuring
P.O. Box 110
Teachers College, Columbia University
New York, New York 10027

National Council for the Social Studies
(NCSS)
Social Education
Social Studies and the Young Learner
3501 Newark Street NW
Washington, DC 20016

National Council of Supervisors of
Mathematics (NCSM)
NCSM Newsletter Leadership in
Mathematics Education
P.O. Box 10667
Golden, Colorado 80401

National Council of Teachers of
English (NCTE)
Language Arts
Primary Voices K-6
1111 Kenyon Road
Urbana, Illinois 61801

National Council of Teachers of
Mathematics (NCTM)
Arithmetic Teacher
Teaching Children Mathematics
1906 Association Drive
Reston, Virginia 22091

National Dance Association
(NDA)
Spotlight on Dance
1900 Association Drive
Reston, Virginia 22091

National Science Teachers Association
(NSTA)
Science and Children
Science for Children: Resources for Teachers
1840 Wilson Boulevard
Arlington, Virginia 22201

Phi Delta Kappa
Phi Delta Kappan
408 North Union
Bloomington, Indiana 47402

Society for Research in Music Education
Journal for Research in Music Education
c/o Music Educators National Conference
1806 Robert Fulton Drive
Reston, Virginia 22091

The Southern Poverty Law Center
Teaching Tolerance
400 Washington Avenue
Montgomery, Alabama 36104

Teachers of English to Speakers of Other
Languages (TESOL)
TESOL Newsletter
1600 Cameron Street, Suite 300
Alexandria, Virginia 22314

The Strategies for Teaching and Learning Professional Library

Administrators Supporting School Change

Robert Wortman

1-57110-047-4   paperback

Bob Wortman is a talented elementary school principal who writes with conviction and humor of his goals and strategies as a principal in this book directed at all who are interested in school revitalization, especially administrators and curriculum supervisors.

Bob explains the importance of having a vision and philosophy as well as a practical understanding of how people learn, an ability to make use of time and organization, and a concern for maintaining positive relationships with all members of the school community—parents, students, and teachers.

Assessment: Continuous Learning

Lois Bridges

1-57110-048-2   paperback

Effective teaching begins with knowing your students, and assessment is a learning tool that enables you to know them. Indeed, the real power of continuous assessment is that it informs your teaching and helps you decide what to do next.

This book provides a wide range of teacher-developed kidwatching and assessment forms to show different ways to reflect on children's work. It offers developmental checklists, student and child interview suggestions, guidelines for using portfolios, rubrics, and self-evaluation profiles. Also included are *Dialogues* that invite reflection, *Shoptalks* that offer lively reviews of the best and latest professional literature, and *Teacher-To-Teacher Field Notes* offering tips from practicing educators.

Creating Your Classroom **Community**

Lois Bridges

1-57110-049-0   paperback

Chances are the teachers you remember are those who really knew and cared for you as an unique individual with special interests, needs, and experiences. Now, as a teacher with your own classroom and students to care for, you'll want to create a classroom environment that supports each student as an individual while drawing the class together as a thriving learning community.

Creating Your Classroom Community offers the basics of effective elementary school teaching:

- how to create a classroom that supports what we know about learning;
- how to help each of your students to develop and practice self-responsibility;
- how to organize your classroom workspace to best support learning;
- how to construct a curriculum that focuses on your teaching and evaluation methods;
- how to turn to parents and the larger community for classroom support.

Dance as a Way of Knowing

Jennifer Zakkai

1-57110-064-4   paperback

Jennifer Zakkai illuminates how and why dance is a powerful tool for creative learning in K–6 classrooms. Student will learn how to engage in structured learning experiences that demand a high level of concentration and creativity. You don't have to be a dancer to enjoy using the detailed model lessons that take your students through warm-ups, movement explorations, rich curricular integrations, culminating activities, observation, and reflection.

Drama as a Way of Knowing

Paul G. Heller

1-57110-050-4   paperback

You don't have to be a Broadway actor to use drama in your classroom. There's plenty of dramatic energy in your students already, and Paul Heller shows you how to turn it into an effective learning tool.

Through his Ten-Step Process in which you, the teacher, are the director, he shows what you should do to guide your students through rewarding dramatic experiences. You'll find out how to use drama techniques to enable students to access and explore the curriculum in ways that promote deeper thinking. Moving beyond techniques, he also presents the nuts and bolts of pantomime and improvisation, of writing and acting scenes, even creating and presenting large-scale productions.

Literature as a Way of Knowing

Kathy G. Short

1-57110-063-6   paperback

Basal programs cannot provide the variety and choice of reading materials that meet students' needs. Stories that are worth reading and that extend children's experiences and enrich their minds also motivate them to make reading part of their lives. Kathy Short outlines the four roles literature plays in the curriculum and shows you how to use real books to help children learn. She concludes with a discussion of evaluation as part of the curriculum and offers specific examples of evaluation techniques and samples of appropriate forms.

Math as a Way of Knowing

Susan Ohanian

1-57110-051-2   paperback

Award-winning author Susan Ohanian conducts a lively tour of classrooms around the country where "math time" means stimulating learning experiences. To demonstrate that mathematics is an active, ongoing way of perceiving and interacting with the world, she explores teaching mathematical concepts through hands-on activities, writing and talking about what numbers mean, and discovering the where and why of math in everyday life.

Focusing on the NCTM's Standards, Susan takes you into classrooms for a firsthand look at exciting ways the standards are implemented. For the nonspecialist in particular, Susan shows that math really is an exciting and powerful tool that students can readily understand and apply.

Music as a Way of Knowing

Nick Page

1-57110-052-0   paperback

Rich with ideas on how to use music in the classroom, *Music as a Way of Knowing* will appeal especially to classroom teachers who are not musicians, but who enjoy and learn from music and want to use it with their students. Indeed, Nick Page reveals the truth of the adage "If you can talk, you can sing. If you can walk, you can dance."

Nick provides simple instructions for writing songs, using music to support learning across the curriculum, teaching singing effectively, and finding good songs. He assures you that with time, all students can sing well. The good news is that once you've read this book, you'll have the confidence to trust yourself—and your students—to sing and learn well through the joy and power of music.

Second Language Learners

Stephen Cary

1-57110-065-2   paperback

Stephen Cary helps K–5 teachers and administrators bring second language learners at all levels of English language proficiency into the core curriculum. With plenty of charts, visuals, and student samples as text support, Stephen shows you that comprehensible, engaging instruction means SSL kids acquire more content and more language. Whether involved in SLL program planning, coordinating staff-development workshops, or teaching in an elementary classroom, you'll find an abundance of ideas in this book.

Writing as a Way of Knowing

Lois Bridges

1-57110-062-8   paperback

You can help your students become flexible writers who understand all that writing can do and who know how to use it to serve their own purposes.

With Lois Bridges as your guide, you'll explore the many ways to develop young writers:

- how to run a writer's workshop;
- how to implement effective mini-lessons;
- how to conduct thought-provoking writing conferences;
- how to handle revising, editing, and publishing;
- how to recognize the qualities of effective writing.

Lois also explains how to teach the basic skills within the context of real writing, and how to help young writers monitor their own use of conventional spelling, punctuation, and grammar. She covers writing as it applies throughout the curriculum in a chapter on students as independent researchers, tracking down, sorting, and presenting data in a wide variety of formats, and outlines a four-step instructional strategy for introducing new genres, including journal writing and poetry.

DATE D'